Blackmen say Goodbye ♀Misery say Hello ♀Love

The Black Man's Alternative to The American Black Woman

By

Yoshua Barak

A&B BOOKS PUBLISHERS
Brooklyn, New York
11201

> ## To My
> ## " New-Reconstruction "
> ## wife, and my two
> ## New world Order Sons

first edition
manufactured in the Unitted States of America

ISBN 1-881316-10-6

ooooo

A&B BOOKS PUBLISHERS
149 Lawrence Street
Brooklyn , New York
11201

(718) 596-3389

FIRST PRINTING 1992

1 2 3   4 5   6 7   8 9 10   11   12

TABLE OF CONTENTS

Chapter	Contents	Page

hard work; pain; five states of a black man's relationship awareness development; black men must reject the American black woman; more failures of the black man; building a black nation; our primary mission; three main predictions on black women.

THE BASIC ARGUMENT

1. Black men and Black women are at war with each other.

2. Black women are miserable obnoxious creatures.

3. The ugly nature of Black Woman is the fault of the Black man. Her hostility is directly related to his ineptness and incompetence.

4. The American Black woman has become the witting and/or unwitting ally of White America in a campaign of destruction of the American Black Man.

5. There will be no significant reconciliation between Black men and Black Women. The great amount of mistrust and hostility between the two will always remain.

6. Black men must change many things about themselves. They have been a passive, inept, weak and poor planners, all of which have caused the Black Woman to be hostile to Black Men.

7. Black men must forget the American Black Woman.

8. Black men must form alliances and finally marry Women from Africa, Asia, or Latin America and from the era of the New-Reconstruction.

9. The **New-Reconstruction** must function independently of White American Society

10. The above arguments are correct . The resulting proposal will work. I know. I've done it.

ACKNOWLEDGEMENTS.

I wish to express my heartfelt appreciation to the following persons who extended themselves on my behalf, even though it may have inconvenienced them. I've used initials to " *Protect the innocent.*"

To:

1. God, who directed me to write this book.

2. I.A whose "black-white" approach to analyzing the world, always gives me clarity.

3. O.P whose absolute loyalty was critical to this project.

4. K.W. whose insights into the publishing business were of great value.

5. D.W who gave me the Black Woman's point of view on the things I wrote.

6. A.T. a real " *needle in the haystack*" black woman who gave me again, a woman's perspective on what I was writing

7. S.D. whose strength to overcome personal set backs in life always served as a model to me.

8. S.R. who provided me with much laughter all during the writing, and who gave me a Spanish woman's perspective on my work. Thanks S.R and stop looking **so good**

9. I.H. another "*needle in the haystack,*" woman who gave some good advice.

10. C.F. whose tireless efforts in the financial realm insured that this book would not go down as another unimplemented "Ethnic" idea.

11. Those majestic Brothers out in L.A who had the guts to take a stand and take a head . "*No justice, no peace.*"

Black male and female relationships are in crises, because the Black race is in crises. **Mr. Barak** ties the survival of the Black race to the fate of the Black male. He sees Black men finding mates, constructing a new world with strong family values, and fighting the white male power structure as a survival imperative. He puts forth the volatile view that African American women are allies of the oppressive power structure and therefore must be replaced in the minds and hearts of their men with women of other worlds.

He points a finger at Black men and Black women equally for the malaise in our communities. However, he puts the burden for dismantling the life long social and economic deformation of Black America squarely on the shoulders of Black males. It is his contention that Black men alone have the moral and historical responsibility to effect change. He argues, this change will only be realized when Black men are united with supportive mates. He feels the vast majority of African American women have been so corrupted by American society, that there is no hope for their collective redemption. Women from Africa, Asia, Latin America and some Caribbean countries are seen as suitable replacements for their *aggressive* and *hostile* American contemporaries.

There is no room in **Mr Barak's** world for well educated independent women. Education viewed as a tool utilized by the power elite to manipulate and control the minds of Black people , particularly Black women. Initially, there will be no place for educated women in the new world constructed by **Mr. Barak** and his followers. Women will serve to raise families, keep the home fires burning, and generally to *"stand by their man"* in Barak 's era of the **New-Reconstruction** as he names it. Women who see themselves in other roles will find **Mr. Barak's** world a hostile environment.

Yoshua is a provocative voice, and a voice that should be heard. He speaks to huge unacknowledged tensions in Black male-female relationships. He expresses opinions and solutions that will excite controversy, spur people to action, or at the very least, reflection. Any Black person who reads this book will begin to question the quality of their relationships, and passionately discuss questions they didn't ask before this intriguing read, This discourse, is exciting and important. **Mr. Barak** certainly adds fuel to the fire, and ignites *"hot debate"* around a topic that has bought years of disappointment and unfulfillment to the many brothers and sisters in bad relationships. I believe intelligent, diverse voices, raised in dialogue about the nature of our relationships, will enable Black America to break the binds that prevent all of us, regardless of gender, from obtaining happiness, harmony and an ascendant role in social structures designed exclusively by Blacks , for their own benefit.

CHAPTER-ONE

Preliminary-Discussion

1

I want to caution you from the very beginning. This book is going to be painful. Black Men, you're going to have to get up some courage to deal with the material we're going to discuss. Many of you are going to be angry at me sometimes and angry at yourselves at other times, but I know when you're finished reading, you're going to thank me for writing this book and thank yourselves for taking the time to read it. You're going to find some portions that you may not agree with but at least you will have had to *THINK*. This book is designed to compel you to think and analyze many different subjects. This book will compel you to dig deep into the nature of your wives, girlfriends, sisters, and mothers. You're going to be doing some heavy soul searching. You'll be digging deepest into your *own* nature as a Black man in America. When we start this self analysis, you're going to have to be courageous. I too, had to muster up courage in order to deal with some aspects of my character and habits as a Black man in America. To use the old cliques of the 1960s, we're going to *"define the problem, talk about the problem then take action"*. When we get through, all the *"real men"* are going to feel better. The Real Men will *feel* better because they'll *be* better. Those Black men who want to remain nothing more than a bunch of chumps, nothing more than clowns, nothing more than passive, slave minded fools, in brief, those Black men who want to continue to be nothing but weak old faggots, will not feel better after reading this book. I will have put a knife in their gut and made them wrench. I will have brought them face to face with the truth about themselves. If you think you're one of those type of men you'd better put the book down right now. I repeat. It won't do you a darn bit of good.

When we're done defining, thinking, and talking,

we'll have a clear understanding of the following;

1. How the Negative nature of the American Black woman, and her effect upon your life, can be neutralized,

2. How shiftless, no count, passive, Black men can transform their characters into productive, wholesome, authoritative, and creatively aggressive commanders,

3. The step by step procedure that a Black man can use to get himself a co-operative mate from Africa, Asia, Latin America and certain Caribbean countries,

4. How the white society's attempt to destroy the Black man can be neutralized.

5. How Black men can say good-bye to misery, say hello to love, and become masters of their homes and of their world around them.

In short gentlemen, I'm going to help you move from the men that many of you <u>are</u>, to the men that you <u>ought</u> to be. **NOW LET'S GO TO IT, DO IT, AND GET IT DONE!**

<u>LET'S REVIEW WHAT</u> <u>WE'VE ALREADY BEEN TOLD:</u>

During the past couple decades, American Black women have been attentive students of the White, Women's Liberation Movement. Black women began to shift from being under your guidance as a Black man, to being under the tutelage of the Women's movement and/or white males. An elderly gentleman told me years ago that for every second of our life, you're under a plan. You're under your own plan or someone else's plan but as sure as day follows night, you'll be under **some** plan. The only question is whose plan. In 1992, American Black women are firmly under the white women's lib plan and the plan of white males. These two white groups are in control of Black women directly and indirectly. They are her masters. American Black women don't have a plan developed *by* them, *for* them, or by Black men, for them (the natural order of things). They're not smart enough to develop one. No woman is smart enough to create a master plan for society. She's a follower. She jumps on board the best plan she can find. It's the old *"I want somebody to take care of me"* syndrome. Women have always thought like this. It's their nature. In spite of the attempt of the Woman's movement to change this, a woman's nature remains essentially the same and it's likely that women will continue to be this way. I'm not complaining. Women are dependents. This has always been the natural order of things and the natural order of the universe is beautiful. In general, women are socially reactionary not creative. Accordingly, it was easier for the American Black woman to jump on board a ship under way, even though it was a ship of fools, rather than build one themselves. The ship she's trying to jump to is the white man's ship. Later in the book we're going to discuss how this happened. Black women have been used by the white women's libbers and used by white males. The relationship between these two white groups and the Black American woman has been lopsided. It's been a perverted relationship. The American Black woman has gained nothing from this relationship that has any lasting value. I saw a program on TV which took a look at the lives of several so-called "professional women" in the Washington D.C. area. Each of them finally wound up saying,

"I don't have a man in my life. I can't seem to keep one. I'd give up all the material things I've gained if I could just get and keep a man".

White society persuaded these women that career and "things" were all a girl should ever want and all she ever needs. Each of those women finally saw the fallacy of that position. In the final analysis that which was *really* important, was that which they had failed to achieve, namely, a wholesome, loving, long term relationship with a man. Latter on we're going to discuss why the American Black woman took the road of material and career development skills as opposed to

3

relationship development skills. We're going to discover how it came to pass that she became the protegee of the women's libbers and white men. We're going to see just how her assumption of that road affected you as a Black man in America. We're going to see the dilemma this road has placed her in and how that dilemma relates to you. We're going to analyze *your* status here in America and try to get a feel of what lies in the future for you. At first the future is going to look grim but we're going to discuss how we can turn that around. We're going to discuss the family unit and how we can accomplish harmonious, productive family structures. At several times during our discussion, you will be called upon to abandon old habits and think in totally new ways. I'm going to define your old habits and thought patterns as being part of the **Old Word Thinking** or **Old World Man**. I'm going to challenge you to shake Old World thinking and become part of the New World, that is part of a **NEW-RECONSTRUCTION**. It'll be a challenge I'm certain you'll accept. In spite of some doom and gloom that may interlace this book, I want you to know that I consider these days, these times, as the most exciting times I can remember or have ever read about. The challenges we face, the dilemmas we face, will demand of us a degree of excellence in our analysis and in our decision making skills, that will astound the nation as it watches us meet our challenges and prevail over difficult situations. Never in the history of our race will we have demonstrated the sort of profound courage our present condition mandates. Gentlemen, I'm going to point you to some opportunities you may never have considered before. We're going to have a good old time in this book. You're going to wind up with some fine looking, humble, co-operative women as opposed to fine looking, but obnoxious, disagreeable, bad attitude American Black woman you have right now. Yeah, we're going to have a good old time in this book. Read on!

Once you accept the arguments and premises I'll be making, you will find yourself subject to a great deal of very harsh criticism, from American Black women. This shouldn't bother you since you're already under criticism from them anyway. The *"Sapphires"* have had nothing good to say about you for decades so you should be used to it by now. But for those Black men who will feel intimidated by the criticisms of Black women, here is your first challenge. Ignore their criticisms. Why? Because their big fat mouths don't mean a dam thing anyway. Her criticisms should be seen for what they are, the white man's put down of you, by surrogate (substitution). We'll go into this idea latter. If you're going to have to hear the criticism of an American Black woman, you might as well be criticized for something worthwhile. I've got something really worthwhile for you. You're going to see what this **"worthwhile"** thing is as we get further along in the book.

Throughout time, people have always had a difficult time accepting truth. They've had a difficult time accepting truth about everything and anything. You'll be called upon to accept some truths about yourselves and your women. Let's not act like the Old testament Jews Isaiah referenced. The prophet Isaiah reported the ancient Jews as saying,

"...Prophesy not unto us right things, speak unto us smooth things, prophesy deceits."[1]

I'm not going to tell you **"smooth things"**. I'm not going to prophesy unto you deceits. I'm going to smack you in the nose with hard facts. Jews were in a constant state of disobedience and rebellion against God. The prophets chastised them constantly, but the people never wanted to be told about their disobedience. They never wanted to hear the truth. They wanted to hear lie. They wanted the prophets to watch their disobedience and say,

"Hey Jew home boys, it's ok to rebel against God. God's word is relative. You can construct your own private interpretations of it and if your interpretations lead you to approving of homosexuality, and disobedient women, why that's ok. Everything's everything. It's all relative you know."

Too often, it took a catastrophe in order to get the Jews to listen to truth. It takes strength to grapple with truth. The truth we're

---

[1]   King James Version (KJV) Isaiah 30:10

focusing on in this book concerns the issue of our relationship with American society in general, and with American Black women in particular. We're also going to have to accept another truth which is that there are things about us, as Black men, that need to change. Just remember what God told Joshua in the Bible;

> "...*Be strong and of good courage; be not afraid, neither be thou dismayed;...*" [2]

Gentlemen, we've got a battle ahead of us but victory is *certain* **if** we choose a victorious path. All we have to do is have the courage to take the courses of action which assure us the final victory. We're going to have to have courage under all circumstances.

Early in the American struggle for independence from British rule, a minister by the name of Simeon Howard gave a sermon calling upon the congregation to produce **"able men"**. In that sermon he said,

> "*By able men, may be intended men of courage, of firmness and resolution of mind, men that will not sink into despondency at the sight of difficulties, or desert their duty at the approach of danger, ...[men] that will not fear the resentment of turbulent, factious men; men that will decide seasonably upon matters of importance, and firmly abide by their decision, not wavering with every wind that blows...*" [3]

Simeon Howard knew the crises of the times required that men, formerly of little consequence, become men of renown. He called upon men absorbed in a world of frivolity and self indulgence, to become men committed to struggle. His call and the calls of others like him were answered. The result is that America is a free nation rather than a British colony today. Today, I make a similar call. I call upon Black men, who

[2] KJV, Joshua 1:9, see also 1:7
[3] Simeon Howard, A.M., of Boston Mass, Election Sermon, 1780 as quoted from They Preached Liberty by Franklin P. Cole p.115

have been of little consequence, to become men of renown. White America, with the help of our own Black women, is trying to destroy Black men. We are called to put aside the frivolity of basketball playing and leave the Super Bowl before the end of the game. We are called upon to become men of struggle. I proceed upon the assumption that we are up to the task.

Some of you won't be inspired to make changes based upon any philosophical, political, or other altruistic arguments. That's ok. But you **will** be motivated to change when you discover that after reading this book, absorbing it's ideas, and making the changes it recommends, there's a good women waiting for you. That's right, I'm dangling a carrot in front of your face. The carrot is going to be a wholesome, lovely, co-operative, polite, dutiful woman. You're going to get her, but only when you're entitled. By entitled, I mean 'prepared'. That's right gentlemen, you have to be prepared to receive a good woman. Most of you have know nothing but miserable bad attitude girls all your life. This experience has corrupted your general outlook on women. You have to be deprogrammed. You have to shake the negative psychological effects of those bad experiences you've had with that American Black woman before you're mentally ready to receive a good woman. We're all going to work together towards that cleansing of our brains and hearts. I'm going to do my best to help you. Yes indeed, when you're finished reading, you'll be ready to replace **obnoxious leg**, with **co-operative leg**. It can really happen gentlemen! I know from first hand experience.

As I just alluded, most of you have never known anything other than raunchy, bad attitude American Black women. The exceptions are those of you who have the opportunity to visit other countries. Veterans know what I'm talking about when I speak of humble beautiful dutiful women. They've experienced it. Most of them regret that they were too young to have realized the good thing they had in their hands while they were stationed overseas. Had they been able to look ahead in time and see how the American girl was going to turn out, they would have married one of the girls in the country where they were serving. You're now faced with the American Black woman. You think that all women are like her. You're going to see that this is not true. So by hook or crook, by the exercise of reason, or the enticement of **"delectable delights"**, I'm going to lead you to some truths that will help you be the man you ought to be, and get that women you ought to have.

2

People with the loudest mouths are the ones who get the most attention even if they shouldn't. The dumbest man on Earth will get more attention and service than you, simply because he's a pain in the rear, and by accommodating him, you can shut him up. I used to watch Jews who had children in school. Man oh man, they were a royal pain in the rear. The Jews were always complaining about this or that. Bitch, bitch, bitch, that's all they did. Teachers and administration hated them *BUT*, the Jews would always get their way. The school felt compelled to placate Jews by satisfying their every whim. When I saw this, I started doing the same thing. I got the school to a point where it hated to see me coming. They just didn't want to deal with my constant complaining. The best way to cool me out was simply to give me what I wanted. So what I wanted was always what I got. My child didn't have to catch some of the stuff other Black kids were catching. The school knew they would have to deal with me. The school didn't want parental involvement for fear of loosing professional control *BUT* when they took a look at the balancing scales, they figured it was far better to loose control with respect to one Black parent (me) in order to keep control over the many. Wise thinking. Raise hell, and you'll make out like a bandit. Be passive and you'll get shit on. You can debate the Jew's methodology, but you can't debate their success. Jews aren't passive. They're active. A passive Jew is a dead Jew. Adolph Hitler taught them this simple truth. Yeah, sometimes it takes a catastrophe to come to grips with truth and reality.

Silent Black people, are ignored Black people. Sometimes it's good to be ignored and unnoticed. Obviously you cannot conduct a covert intelligence gathering operation if you're noticed. But sometimes it's good to be listened to. When a man comes in the office with a really good idea but speaks softly, no one pays attention to him. But the ambitious guy who talks loud, speaks bull, and on occasion uses ten dollar words, will be admired and thought of as a genius. He gets the raises and the promotions. Mr. Quiet nice guy, smart as a whip, gets fired if he takes too long a drink at the water fountain. Gentlemen, it's our turn as Black men to start shouting. We've been silent for entirely too long. Our silence has had a incredibly damaging effect upon may aspects of lives here in America, in particular, the character of our relationships with Black women. We have to get active. We have to start to speak up and speak out. Black men as a group are too darn passive. In 1992 you can still kick a Black man in the shin and he'll say thank you. Often our passivity and our silence is construed as *"consent"* to the adverse things happening to and around us. Our silence in the face of the women's movement was construed as a tacit approval of that movement. We should never have been silent, passive. I asked a lady from the island of Barbados what she thought were the differences between men in Barbados and American Black men. She told me that Bajan men were aggressive but American Black men were *"calm"*. She clarified the word *"calm"* by advising me that she meant **"passive"**. There was much she liked about American men, but she expressed grave concern about our passive nature. She said that the passive nature of American Black men made her feel insecure. Gentlemen, we have to get "constructively active". Excluding the murderous activity of young Black men and teenagers who are shooting each other full of holes, everybody has been active except us. White men have been active. They've been actively kicking our tails for centuries. White women have been active. They've been developing and implementing the Women's Lib program for decades. Black women have been active. They've become the active allies of whites in a campaign against us. They're actively engaged in conspiracies to wreck Black men's lives.

Yes indeed, the Back woman knows how to open her mouth and get attention. She's been running her fat mouth for decades, *"shoutin loud"*. Every time you turn around, there's a Black woman with her hands on her hips, mouth open, talking nonsense. These days she's talking the women's lib nonsense. She also believes she's the expert of experts. She

9

wants to tell Harold Katz how to run the Sixer's and General Powell how to run the army. If Albert Einstein were alive today, she'd want to tell him how to do his physics. I can't count the times some Black woman has asked me a question and then given me an argument about my answer. She asked because she didn't know. Suddenly she becomes an expert and disputes my answer without having any basic knowledge in the area of her question. Why bother to ask me anything at all? I know a great deal about computers. A Black woman who never touched one in her life asked me advice on what to look for when buying one. For each thing I told her she had an argument against it. She finally went to a white boy and asked the same questions. The white boy was selling an obsolete line of computers and told her all sorts of lies and garbage in order to get her to make a purchase. She took the white boy's advice because he was white. She bought the obsolete computer. Not only was it obsolete, it was totally inadequate for her purposes. She then had the nerve to come back to me and ask for help. She was unrepentant. I told her I'd be glad to help her as soon as I received confirmation that it was snowing in Hell. I suggested that she visit the region personally, and try sending me a report on the weather down there. I'd make sure she carried a pair of snow boots. I wouldn't want her to catch the flu you know. I was an expert, but the white boy was white. In her mind, whiteness meant expertise. With expertise, he duped her into buying a piece of junk.

Yeah, the Black woman keeps her mouth running and nothing comes out but loud noise, trash, and hard times. Well if she can get away with running her mouth about bull, we should be able to run our mouths abut truth. It's the Black man's turn to speak now. It's our turn to talk truth instead of trash. You're about to receive some truth. You're going to hear the hard biting, rock bottom, acid facts. To test whether what I will say is true or not, simply ask yourself "Is what Barak saying reflect my own experiences in life and with Black women in particular?". While I was writing this book, I'd take a breather and show some of the chapters to both men and women. The real men were saying,

"un huh, that's right, the brother's talkin the real thing now".
``

There were a few, misguided, pro-feminist Black men, who in their best professor voice would say,

"Well, I think your book is rather inflammatory. Can't you say these things in a way that won't be so offensive to women? You know what they say, you can catch more bears with honey than with vinegar."

Well, Professor Scum F. Pervert, let me at the vinegar! I don't want to catch any of these 'bears'. Yes indeed, keep the booga-bears away from me! Sometimes I'd hear these misguided men say;

"Well, I think you're being unfair to women. Women have made many strides in the past decade and we have to do all that we can do to lend them support."

Gentlemen, you can guess what I was thinking as I listened to these poor misguided idiots. I know you can guess it. I can hear your thoughts. They're the same ones I had. I'm still trying to figure out what strides Professor Pervert was talking about. The only stride I can think of is that new long stride women's libbers use when they're trying to walk like a man. These Black men are nothing more than a bunch of duped chumps. Their women probably have them under thumb. Actually the phrase "their women" is a contradiction in terms. Such men don't have any women. Women have them instead! These are the kind of Black men who women call "sweet" and show off at parties. The men smile and act like chumps and the women get in huddles to discuss how good a job this or that Ms. Sapphire did in turning him into a worm. Such women are probably out screwing other men, real macho men. They'll keep the chump around just to take his money and otherwise use him, but they'll turn to a real macho man (if they can find one) on the side.

Yes gentlemen, we've lost control of our women. We

11

only THINK we're in control. We want to go around fooling ourselves and saying we are, but in fact we're not. If you want to keep giving yourself this bull, you'd better put this book down right now. You've wasted your money. You're not going to get anything out of it but I'm glad I got your cash, chump. The women are taking your money and wasting it. I might as well take it and use it for my own good and the good of real men. See me next year when you're ready to stop being crapped on by Black women and start acting like a man. Meanwhile, my next piece of carrot cake is on you. Yes sir, this book is only for real men, able to face real truths and make some real changes.

3

As I said, American Black women have become agents of white society against your interest as Black men. They've been used by the White Women's Libbers as in the case of Anita Hill's accusations against Clarence Thomas during his Supreme Court Confirmation Hearings. Black women have formed an unholy alliance with white people, the purpose of which is to denigrate and destroy Black men. That's right gentlemen. Black women want to destroy Black men. They hate us with a passion. Whites put the Black woman's hatred to good use. White men feel threatened by Black men. They feel we are superior. If they don't repress us, they think we'll turn around, kick them in their ass, and take everything back they've taken from us, plus some extras. They're probably right. I know I'd bust them down to less than a nickel, given half the chance. The future security of white men depends on keeping Black men in the dumps. This is their divine duty as they see it. White men fear what they call **"The Browning of America"**. They're afraid of

1. The current wave of non-white immigration into America,
2. The increase in Black birth rates,
3. Easy access for white women to abortion clinics.

White males are vehemently opposed to white women having easy access to abortions. White women aborting pregnancies coupled with an escalating non white birth rate

12

doesn't do much good for white male's sense of security. The **Browning of America** would be further encouraged under such conditions. There are already areas of the country in which whites are the minority. Miami, as an example, could be appropriately named **New Cuba**. U.S. Government statistics give a projection of what the American population will look like from now until the year 2025 based upon current trends in birth and death rates reflected in the Census data. These statistics project a substantial increase in the percentage of the population that will be non white, black and Spanish in particular during the coming century. The figures project an escalating increase in the birth rates of non whites while by comparison only a minor increase in the white birth rate.[4] Whites are afraid that by the close of the 21st century or even earlier, America will become a brown nation if the current trends are not halted. In other words, the Pilgrims will have come all the way over here for nothing and the Colonist will have died in vain because the U.S.A. got "down and brown". Accordingly, in the minds of George Bush, Pat Buchanan, David Duke, and most other *"responsible"* white men, You (Black People) Must Be Stopped!

99I have always been amazed by the Integrationist movement. The whole thing never made sense to me. It's a bit bizarre that Black men went to their enemy and asked for help.

[4]   Statistical Abstract of the United States, 1991, The National Data Book, U.S. Dept. of Commerce, Bureau of Census, Charts # 14, 15, 16, 17 ,18. Appendix A, Table 11, shows the gradual increase in the population of non whites over a 39 year period. The table shows the corresponding decrease in the percentage of whites making up the total population. Table 17 projects the years 1995 to 2025. The percent net Increase column projects a significant difference between white and black population rate increases. Net increases of non whites occurs at a rate roughly 2 1/2 to 3 times faster than whites. Appendix B, Table 14 shows similar data for the years 1960 to 1989. Again, the rate of non white births generally exceeds that of whites. Appendix C was useful for analyzing the percentage change of the population by a more refined specification but also includes race as a factor. This projection is still consistent with those of Appendices A and B. It suggest an increase in the non white birth rates exceeding that of the white population

13

How in the world can you expect your enemy to help **YOU** defeat **THEM** and finance the effort too. When you're this . ridiculous, all you will deserve and no doubt get, is a swift kick in the rear. This is part of the reason why our women are hostile to us. Deep down inside they resent the fact that all we have done is beg the white man for a place in the sun, in his back yard. This is what integration is, organized begging. It's not respectful. No integrationist is respectful. Women want to respect men. They want to look up to a man and see him as ultimate power. If all we can do is grovel at the foot of the Washington Monument to beg for a Civil Rights bill that expires at the whim of the white man, we don't look like powerful men, just sophisticated beggars. We're going to address this again a bit latter. We're going to see that Black women went over to where they perceived power was.

As I said, the security of white men depends on us living in a state of confusion and turmoil. White America feels good when they see us killing each other, drugged up, or better yet, wasting our time day and night arguing with some ignorant, obnoxious Black women. White society has encouraged Black women to be precisely that way. **BUT**, we've had a role in this encouragement too. Yeah, the American Black woman is the agent of the white man. Ms. Sapphire, hot and sassy, doing all she can to work a red hot knife up and down your spine.

Gentlemen, we must re-establish control over women and our households. In order to accomplish this, we must first understand that it **SHOULD** be accomplished. If you don't believe you should be the senior ranking officer in your relationship, you **WON'T** be. And if you're not, don't complain when your raunchy Black woman runs all over you. You'll have deserved it. You're getting what you believe in, namely, command authority for your woman and subservience for you! You're probably a believer in the equality of men and women. You probably believe in Women's Lib. You're the sort of Black man that's a misguided, weak, pervert. You have a distorted notion of what constitutes truth. You've bought a bill of goods hook line and sinker, in particular the women's Lib bill of goods. Men like you are a national disgrace. Your entire lives are spent sucking up to your women, groveling at their feet. You defer to her most capricious, extravagant, frivolous, and irrational wish. You men belong to the **Chumps of America Brigade.** But don't worry. I'm going to do you "C.A.B.'s" a favor and point you to some truths. I'm going to try to "unchumperize" you. I'll lead you to the water trough but I won't try to force you to drink. We are all what we decide to be. Once you've been told the truth and you still decide to keep your membership in the C.A.B., well, that's on you.

2

As Black men, we need to start thinking of alternatives to the American Black woman. If she can't get her act together and be humble and co-operative, if she can't keep that nasty mouth of hers shut, if she can't see her primary responsibility as a wife and homemaker, she ought to be left behind in the dust with her white masters. Let her discover how much of a friend whites will be. Let the white man deal with her negative nature for a change. The Black woman will be in for a real surprise when her masters look her square in the face and say,

"Go to hell. Your men have wised up. They've stopped taking your disrespect. They've stopped getting into arguments with you. We can't use you any more against them. They've gotten smart. They've caught on to our game. Now, Black girl, you're of no use to us. You're no good to your own men. We know because we trained you how to give them nothing but a hard time. Now you're no good to us either. Get away. Go take a shit in a broken toilet seat".

Black men will have to understand that the American Black woman isn't the only woman on the planet. You have more to choose from. You can look elsewhere. You **SHOULD** look elsewhere! You want a decent, appreciative, calm, dutiful, respectful, loyal Black Woman? Look to Africa. Look to Asia. Look to Latin America and the Caribbean islands. I know this is what you want. All during the writing of this book Black men would say to me,

15

"Hey man where's that chapter on Options. I heard you gonna tell us about some decent women we can have. Man, let me in on the How To Do It part. I'm tired of these sick Black bitches here. I want a change."

I heard this over and over again. I tell you, thousands of Black men all across America are saying this and asking for options to the American Black woman. Well hold on to your hats gentlemen. I hear you! I know you're thirsting to get rid of that terrible American Black woman of yours. We'll get to that in due time. I promise I'll discuss it in the chapter on Options.

3

The divorce rate in America is alarming. Over 50% of all marriages are failing before the first two years are up. The rate has been steadily increasing since the 1960's. This increase in divorce comes right at a time that the Women's Liberation movement took full force. The Women's Lib movement spelled the death kneel for harmonious, loving, male-female relationships in American society between white men and white women. It's now spilled over to Black men and women. It got some women those careers they wanted so much, but it backfired on them in other ways. It backfired on them in the way that really counts for a woman, male-female relationships. The women of the 90's see themselves as "free, independent, career women" but all they've achieved is the **illusion** of freedom and the **reality** of loneliness.

Years ago, a most distinguished, elderly gentleman told me that *"a woman's whole life is a man"*. A woman without a man is one of the most miserable creatures on this planet and friends, we've got millions of miserable, angry women walking around. I call them **D.O.B.'s**, *"Daughters of Bitches"*. The Black ones are the absolute worse of the bunch. When a Black woman is not with a Black man, she's a miserable creature. She becomes more angry and hostile with each passing day. I was watching an old *"Cavalry chases the Indians"* movie. I was half asleep. Everything was going fine until the captain of the troops said something about the *"hostiles"* approaching. Man,

I jumped out of my chair and broke into a cold sweat. For a second or two, the word 'hostiles' made me think some hostile Black women were approaching. It took me a few seconds to realize that it was only a cable movie playing. I tell you, I was all ready to take out my anti D.O.B. kit and go into combat mode. Nothing's more pathetic than a hostile American Black woman. When they put their hands on their hips and begin talking their trash, you've got a real mess to contend with. When this occurs, your options get mighty slim. They narrow down to walking away, kicking her in her ass, or a combination of the two. I saw one American Black girl push and shove her face right up to the nose of a Black man. She was just carrying on, showing off in front of her girlfriends. Her mouth was running loud and wild, a mile a minute. There was more filth coming out of it than an elephant has crap. She was pointing her finger and pushing him back up against a wall. Well she pushed just one time too much. He hauled off and punched her in the jaw. The girl had a nerve to say,

"Ain't no man should hit a woman".

Well she was right, in part, because I say,

"Ain't no man supposed to hit a decent woman but if she's going to jump in a man's face like a man, she should expect to get busted like a man.".

That Black woman jumped in the brother's face like a man would do. Therefore she got what one man will give another, a kick in the ass. How dare she think that the universal law of cause and effect, reaction and counter reaction didn't apply to her. Well let me apologize because I'm sure she doesn't think that anymore. I'm sorry baby. I forgot you got busted in the jaw. That raunchy Black woman was a prime example of a woman that lost her femininity. In her passion to see herself as equal to a man, she took on the attitude and mannerisms of a man. She probably believed she was a man. That girl must have had accelerated levels of testosterone, the male hormone, in her body. She ought to keep away from the Spa and stop reading those women's lib manuals on feminist urban guerilla warfare. They make a woman become more like a man in her character. The hypocrisy is that these women are quick to call themselves your equals and try to act the part, but when they get busted they fall back on their womanhood like the girl I just mentioned. Well, ladies, if you want to walk like a duck, act like a duck and talk like a duck, don't be surprised when you're brought down like a duck in hunting season. You want to act like one of the boys, then don't complain when you get treated like one of the boys.

Many "Afro-Centric" men and members of the **CHUMPS OF AMERICA BRIGADE**, with their perverted pro-feminist perspective, will hate me saying all this. They'll hate it when I tell them that Black American women, at this point in history, constitute the most evil and degenerate subset of humanity known to exist. I can hear the Brigade now, *"Aw he just hates Black women, he's got a mental problem"* etc. Well gentlemen, by the time we get to the end of this book, you'll see the absurdity of such a criticism. Black women, and their misguided Brigade *"comrades in foolishness"*, **love** to tell you that **YOU'RE** the one with a mental problem because you're telling the truth about the ugly nature of the American Black woman. Men, you don't have a mental problem because you want respect, peace, courtesy, co-operation, and someone who genuinely shows concern for you. Idiots who criticize you that way are the ones with the mental problem. In their own individual relationships they may accept abuse, but don't you do it. Somehow in the mire of their perverted thinking, peace and happiness are more than what a Black man has a right to ask for. They accuse you of being insecure. Gentlemen, when you are accused of this, plead guilty! Respond with

"Wow, you're very observant. Yes, I am insecure. Any man who takes a beast into his home and doesn't feel insecure is a complete fool. Such a man is destined to be chewed up by that beast. I suggest to you that you had better start feeling insecure too".

The problem with the *Brigade* is that the poor dumb

bastards ***don't*** feel insecure. They've taken so much abuse from these American Black women that they've begun to think disrespect is normal and acceptable. But we won't worry about them gentlemen. They're not reading this book which means that they'll just have to continue to suffer. They're not ready for prime time.

Gentlemen, as I said at the outset, this book is not for everybody. It's certainly not for weak hearted chumps, and pro feminist scum like Phil Donahue and Black men stupid enough to subscribe to '**Donahue liberalism**'. It's only for those of you willing to accept truth and make a change. If you can't take anything I've said so far, put this book down now! Throw it in the trash. I want you to throw it in the trash. Maybe some homeless person might find it, read it and transform his life into something worth while. I've a lot more to say and it's often as unsettling as what's already been said. But remember, we're going to work this problem through. Much of the criticism I levy against Black men, I also levied against myself at one time or another. None of us are exempt from being adversely affected by our experiences in America. But we're going to come out of this whole discussion relatively happy. We're going to feel challenged. Hopefully we'll take on the challenges I'll put in front of you. We're all going to feel better *"by and by"*. The real men have hung in there so far. Alright, let's get on with it. Let's get on with some truth.

CHAPTER-TWO

White Plan + Hostile Black Woman+
Black Male Apathy = Hell on Wheels

1

Men, you're in one hell of a mess at this point in history. You've been asleep on the job and you need a good shot of truth to wake you up. I spoke with a young man recently who told me that "Our women need to be kicked in the ass". I'll concede that he is correct but before *that* should happen, *Black Men* need to be kicked in the ass. You've a share in the problems you're facing. You've been "enablers", to use today's popular term. I believe that ninety percent of your relationship problems with Black women are the result of your failure to be aware of the changes she was undergoing as a consequence of her adherence to Women's Liberation doctrines. The Black women underwent a metamorphosis. Butterflies undergo the same thing. They turn from unsightly larva and pupae stages to that lovely butterfly. Black women went though a reverse metamorphosis. They were graceful, lovely and dutiful and have turned into the disagreeable, disgraceful degenerates they currently are. Its taken her a long time to undergo this metamorphosis. It happened all the while you were playing football and basketball instead of monitoring her and her associates (I tell you, give a Black man a basketball and he'll forget not only world hunger, but the fact that his own butt is starving). You weren't paying close attention to the little tell tail words and phrases she began to adopt like *"sisterhood"*, *"independent"*, *"options open"* and *"whole person"*. When she started saying things like *"liberation for women means men will also be free"* a red flag should have gone up in your head.. You failed to grasp the far reaching effect Women's Liberation would have on male-female relationships in America. Slowly but surely, your woman began to absorb its doctrines to the specific detriment of your relationship. When that Black woman of yours came into the house talking about being independent, you should have straightened her out right then and there, on the spot. You should have made it clear to her at that instant in time, she was free to "independent herself right out the door". You should have let her know that if you ever heard her talk this trash again you would help her pack her bags. If either partner in a relationship see themselves as independent, there is no basis for the survival of that relationship other than sex. Sex as the sole basis for sustaining a marriage or otherwise serious relationship is insufficient. Where either of the parties thinks they are, or should be, independent of the other, a spirit of cooperation and unified purpose is lost. If a woman is independent of you, it means she doesn't need you. I've heard Black men say *"but I like my woman's independence"*. Invariably they wind up saying to themselves, *"darn she treats me like I'm a piece of shit. She acts like she don't need me at all"*. Well, she doesn't! She was independent when you became involved with her and really didn't in any practical sense, feel a need for you beyond sex. She still doesn't feel she needs you. There was never a meaningful unified purpose which bound the two of you together from the start. She was an *"independent woman of the 90's"*. She was doing her thing and you were doing yours. You came together at night for a quickie. That's all there was to it. Why did you get married? Why were the two of you living together? What was that common goal the two of you shared. It didn't exist and so the basis for a relationship never existed. If she started the relationship off with a sense of unity but degenerated afterwards into feeling independent, that's worse. She began by seeing you as being needed but then **"progressed"** to thinking you nothing more than an unwanted appendage, a nuisance. In a relationship of this character, you ought not to be surprised when you don't get out of it loyalty, respect, duty, etc. It either wasn't designed to be about those things from the very beginning or has suffered an erosion of these qualities along the way. Whether you want to admit it or not, such relationships exist only for the purpose of a convenient sex partner. They are little more than what you might arrange with a boardwalk whore. A marriage must be formed by two individuals who can achieve together, what they can not achieve, or find very difficult to achieve separately. The man and woman must have a sense of life long commitment to goals that are better served when two people's efforts are coordinated. If this is not the case, then the whole thing is on rather tenuous grounds. In other words, you're probably going to get crapped on. I've heard women's libbers preach that a woman doesn't need a man for anything. I've head them preach that women should begin to give themselves orgasms and make use of sperm banks if they want to get pregnant. In one well known organization whose leadership consist primarily of women's libbers, there is a high incidence of lesbianism. Lesbianism is sure to follow where women believe they don't need, and can be independent from, men. Unfortunately this organization spreads feminist doctrines to teen and pre-teen girls. These young girls will become infected with this trash.

2

Don't be fooled. The woman's movement had an objective in mind. The objective, contrary to what the "Libbers" represented it to be, was never the equality of the sexes. The objective was to replace male authority with female authority and thereby dominate men. Black women have been reaping the benefits of the work laid down by the early bra burners. The American Black *"independent"* woman, just like her white counterpart, doesn't want equality. She wants to **dominate** Black men. When a woman dominates, you can bet your behind, that one or another form of chaos is certain to occur. There will be no decisions made calmly, orderly, and rationally. Everything will be tainted by her emotions. A plan will not go as well as it might have gone, and probably won't jump off at all.

As I suggested earlier, American Black women have begun to subscribe to the doctrines and philosophy of the white Women's lib movement of the 1960's. Black women weren't on the forefront of the demonstrations of that time period, but they're reaping the so called *"benefits"* at this point in history. Black women are the beneficiaries of the woman's movement. They're lapping up the slop the white girls laid down. During the 1960's Black women were more inclined to

see their role as one of support for Black men engaged in the
"Black Liberation Struggle" as it was called then. I have vivid
recollections of Black women, on more than one occasion,
telling white women that there was a distinction to be made
between the needs of the women's liberation movement and
the **Black Liberation** movement. Black women had enough
insight to realize that the women's movement's goal was
separation from men. It was hostile to men. Young Black
women of the 1960's felt the need to grow closer to Black men
who were under assault by, and being murdered by, the police
forces of the nation. These forces in turn were acting as agents
for, and on behalf of, the U.S. Government. The Black
Movement, of the 1960's, mandated unity between Black men
and women. Black women back then, had no time for any
organized effort, such as the white Women's movement, whose
operational philosophy would result in a nonproductive, destructive tension between men and women, the likes of which
we see today.

The organized women's movement is a potent force.
It has eroded many men's confidence in themselves. It's
unbelievable. Trash ideas eroded the confidence of men, as
opposed to men dispelling the trash ideas. You've got men like
Phil Donahue preaching the women's lib line. He'll tell you in
a second how equal women are to men. The truly amazing
thing is that lots of men buy this bill of goods without question.
Ask Phil or any other misguided pervert to prove this equality
and they'll fail. One Black man said to me *"well men and
women can perform the same task so they're equal"*. I asked
him if a seeing eye dog can guide a blind man across the street.
I then asked him if he could guide a blind man across the
street. I then asked him if the dog was then his equal. Likewise
I asked him if monkeys could peel bananas and if he could peel
bananas. I then asked him if a monkey was his equal. Though
he understood the point of my questions and saw the fallacy
of these unsupported claims of equality between things and in
particular between men and women, he walked away really
upset. He wanted to believe Phil Donahue and Gloria Stein-
man. I'd shown his gods to be subject to erroneous thinking.
I feel confident however, that within a few hours after we spoke,

he forced himself to forget our conversation and retrogressed to his old degenerate thinking patterns. Well done Phil, *you've got another nigger in the bag.* The fact that women perform task in the factories has nothing to do with the issue of equality of the sexes. Outside the area of mathematics, you can't show the equality of anything, not even identical twins. However if you can show me that as of tomorrow night, all men will be born with a penis **and** a vagina, and all women will be born with the same, I'll begin to reconsider by position on the equality of the sexes. Until then, I'll say without reservation that,

There has never been in the past, neither is there presently, nor is there likely to be in the future, any women I would see as my equal.

Someone asked me once "*what about the Virgin Mary*"? I like to crap in my pants because I was so disgusted with this idiot. I told him that Jesus himself didn't think much of her and certainly never recognized her as his mother. As a matter of fact, right before his death he gave her away as it were. If Jesus didn't place her on a pedestal, I'll be dammed if I will.

The American Black woman has adopted the white woman's lib philosophy and wields it like a sword pointed right at your throat. She's telling you that she's your equal and that there's no difference between you and her. Some of you men think these dumb ideas in her head will just disappear if we Black men just ignore her. If we just ignore her and let her shoot off her mouth and talk this trash in front of our sons, everything will be ok. Well let me tell you something gentlemen, it won't be ok! A child raised up on trash talk will turn into trash. The book of Proverbs says,

"Train up a child in the way he should go; and when he is old, he will not depart from it." [5]

The belief that men and women are equal and that there isn't any significant difference between the sexes is

_____
[5]   Prov. 22:6

25

absurd! Not only is it absurd, *it's a criminal assault on the concept of sound reasoning*. It's a real tragedy that too many men get intimidated by the women's libbers and become reluctant to openly declare Libber trash as precisely what it is, **TRASH** with a double capital "T". Deep down inside they know these views are insane, but they're afraid of the reaction they'll get from women if they challenge their ridiculous feminist beliefs. Gentlemen, it's disgraceful for Black men to be intimidated this way. It's disgraceful for Black men to allow their women to absorb these ideas and bring them into the house. Black men have to learn to stand tall and soldier! We've got to learn that truth is truth, and that it's usually plain and simple. Trash ideas are trash ideas and trash belongs on the garbage truck not in the house.

I received a copy of a flyer from an organization called the International Black Woman's Congress [6] . The flyer begins in large bold lettering with,

"POLITICAL SOCIALIZATION OF BLACK WOMEN: EMPOWERMENT"

It continues with little goodies such as;

**"LEARN HOW TO TAKE CONTROL OF YOUR LIFE AND RELEASE THE POWER WITHIN!...
COME AWAY FROM THIS CONFERENCE
WITH YOUR ACTION PLAN"**
also;

> *"As we approach the 21st century no topic is more germane to the survival of African American women than that of EMPOWERMENT-..."*

In the vision of this organization for the next century, there is no place for Black men. The flyer never once mentioned Black men. It included no hint of a discussion of Black women working **together** with Black men towards a common goal.

[6]   International Black Woman's Congress, Conference proceedings Sept 27th 1992, Newark New Jersey

Latter in this book we will explore why this is so and what we ought to be doing as Black men to counter act this. The conference list Black women speakers national and international who all have one agenda in mind. It's to prevent men in general, Black men in particular from ever obtaining even the slightest quantum of power for himself. These women echo with identical wording the early battle cry of the white woman's liberation movement. In the flyer they complain about the mass media portraying them unfavorable. The flyer says;

"The mass media has defined Black women in ways that are negative, thus making it difficult for us to define ourselves from our own perspective...We must create our own images"

On face this seems innocent. It seems like an honest cry for dignity. Closer inspection will reveal that is certainly a cry for dignity for Black women but not for Black men. These women could care less about any Black man. Their aim is to look all around America, see what it has to offer **them**, put the pressure on, and grab al they can grab for **themselves**. They are not interested in mass media's negative portrayal of you. They're not interested in your economic or political empowerment. They're out for themselves. They're learning the white girls tricks and intend formally and openly to denigrate you in deference to their own selfish interest. Such women are a lost cause. They are also your adversaries. It has never been more important that Black men parley amongst themselves, form unions, and define themselves and their own agenda. Once defined, we should "carry with us" women who are willing to serve our interest which is to say, the interest of the race in general. This is in marked contrast to the International Black Woman's Congress whose interest does not extend past the Black woman uniquely.

I want you men to take note that the IBWC calls for woman to develop an *"Action Plan"*. Gentlemen, as I may have already mentioned, everybody is active except us, that is Black men. Everybody has an action plan except us. We've allowed ourselves to be distracted with sports and other forms of entertainment. The general policy of white men and now of Black women is to *"Entertain the Black man while we conspire and take action to further subdue him"*. To the extent that we are distracted, it is our own fault for being so inept as to **allow** ourselves to be distracted and defeated.

I wouldn't trust a hostile woman's libber, white or Black, around my sons to save my life. I want my sons to grow up knowing that they are men. I want them raised knowing that their function is to, provide, protect, and command. These are their specific duties. A woman's responsibilities are different. My sons will not be taught some nonsense totally unsupported by the historical record, namely that women and men are equal or that there are no specific obligations unique to each gender. We've got thousands of years of men and women having a clear idea of their capabilities and responsibilities. Now all of a sudden in America, during the last twenty or thirty years in particular, people are talking some mess about equality and androgyny [7]

As unpopular as it may be in these times to say it, the fact is that women are strictly emotional creatures. They are RULED by their emotions. There's not one shred of a stable, rational character in them. Decisions made emotionally are never good decisions. This is why women make so many bad decisions. Men are more dispassionate. They're cool, collected, except for members of the Brigade. One lady friend of mine said to me;

"The difference between men and woman is one of emotions and conduct. You can look at the conduct of a man and get a good idea of the quality of his intellect. A man who acts stupid IS stupid. But you can't look at a woman's conduct and determine her intellect. Women never act consistent with their body of knowledge. Women will continue to get beat up, stabbed and otherwise abused by their man and stay until he kills her. When you ask the woman why she stays she'll say its

---

[7] This refers to the idea of being sexless. Androgynous clothing is designed to be worn by men and women so that the clothing alone does not indicate sex.

because she loves him, or it for the sake of the kids or some other nonsense. She's being destroyed. She should leave. Leaving is consistent with survival but her emotions stand in the way of proper judgment. She is often as bright as anything out there, but bright as she may be, her behavior doesn't suggest it at all. You can't look at a woman's behavior and get a good idea of her intellect. Because of emotions, stupid women act stupid, and bright women act stupid."

When she told me this, I was floored. It rang true. Her conclusion was that men had to be in control of things. She's a born again Christian and said that it was solid scripture that women ought not to be in control. You could count on a man's consistency, if not his brilliance. With women, you could count on nothing but chaos, confusion and irrationality. With American Black women, you have to factor in obnoxiousness, greed, a rebellious spirit, indifference, disrespect and an overall hostility to Black men.

It is at best, the prerogative of a woman to make suggestions and even then, she shouldn't be in the habit of making them too often. It is not her prerogative to control, rule, or ever be the final decision maker over men. Command and control is the sole prerogative of the man. Only **he** is capable of command in any rational and objective way. If the electorate of this nation should ever be so misguided as to choose a woman for president, you'd better believe she's going to be flanked by men who will be calling the shots. It'll be that way or she'll go down in history as part of the shortest lived administration the country has ever seen. White men are not going to let some woman with PMS screw up a major international crises. I can't conceive of the Joint Chiefs permitting World War-III to jump off because some woman on her monthly can't think straight. During the last days of the Nixon Administration, the Pentagon issued orders to all commanders that they were not to obey any orders coming from Nixon. Any such orders had to be first cleared through the Joint Chiefs. This was astonishing. It constituted a mutiny on the part of the highest military authorities in the nation, against their Commander In Chief who they thought would do something as rash as surround and arrest the members of the Senate thereby halting the move to impeach him. Now if these white boys did this to Nixon, what do you think they'd do to a woman on her monthly.

As I said before, at this moment in history, American Black women are the absolute pits of humanity. These obnoxious, hostile Black women are the perfect agents of the white man. They're the most effective weapon the white man has. He uses them against *you.* When white men deny Black men equal opportunity within the framework of a white dominated society, and at the same time send messages to Black women that a man is not a man unless he furnishes you with that new fur coat, and that $300,000 house, knowing full well that the Black man is not able to provide these things, he encourages Black women to think their men are inept. The Black woman never had the smarts enough *not* to fall for a standard of value which was strictly materialistic (it's unfortunate that too many Black men have been equally guilty). A materialistic value system is precisely what it implies. It is a system of evaluating and assigning worth to material objects. There is absolutely nothing wrong with this in and of itself. Where then does the problem lie? It arises when we use the material value method to analyze the *character* of men. This mistake is tantamount to attempting to use a weighing scale as a device for measuring the distance between New York and Philadelphia. The weighing scale has no applicability when it comes to measuring the distance between two points. It's using the wrong tool to do the job. Weight and distance are *valid* concepts but *different* concepts. Likewise, if you use as a measuring device for determining human character, the number of cars a man has, you are mixing your devices or I should say tools. The number of cars a man has may be an indication of many things but it's not a measure of good or bad character. In Philadelphia, Gary Heidnick drove a fancy car and impressed a lot of young Black girls. They all accepted his personal invitation to a home cooked meal and cocaine After entering his house the girls experienced physical abuse, rape, being chained to walls and held as prisoners, and being forced into cannibalism. He drove a fancy car but was he a man of fine character. His car was sufficient evidence of goodness in the minds of those poor unfortunate fools. They learned the hard way about the inapplicability of the material value method as a measuring device for human character. I can see them now, in hell debating the subject.

The material value method applied erroneously as a measurement of human character was contrived by the merchant class. If you can be persuaded that the good man has five objects and the man with only one object is not a good man, then you increase the likelihood that men will buy five objects in order to evidence their goodness. Let me make it clear to you that I accept the material value method as an indication of how comfortable one is likely to be or not be. It's useful for that purpose. If a woman looks at a man with one house and another man with no house, she can reasonably assume that in the one instance she will be dry when it rains and in the other instance she will be uncomfortable. Her use of a material value method as a device to determine the likelihood, or not, of comfort is appropriate. Yet upon this same measuring device alone, she could not determine if either man was a righteous or unrighteous individual. The Black woman accepts the material value method as a legitimate device to measure the character of a man. She applies it to Black men. Black men will usually fail the test in her own mind. Therefore, it will follow in her mind that Black men aren't shit. It never occurs to the Black women that she is using a method to evaluate character that is not designed to evaluate character at all. Furthermore the material value standard, as implemented in America, is far too relative a device to be useful even for the purpose to which it is appropriate. The standard changes every few years. Yesterday the standard may have been "a good man has two Cadillac cars". Today the standard may be "a good man has two BMW's". Tomorrow it may be "a good man has three Benzes, five Rolexes, a winter, spring, summer and fall home". The standard changes and the stakes go up with each change. It doesn't matter that men with Volkswagons shoot their wives and men with BMW's shoot their wives. I guess in a woman's mind, the bullet from the gun of the VW man kills, but the bullet from the gun of the BMW man only stings you a bit. Lord knows, I'll never understand it!

The standard is not only relative, and always increasing in magnitude, it also encourages women to be unappreciative. I know one Black married couple whose marriage is about to break up. They have one child about 4 years old. He recently purchased a four bedroom house for the family. His wife has given him hell ever since. She's complaining that the house is not a five bedroom house like the one her girlfriend has. It doesn't matter that at the age of 37, she's decided that she'll have no more children so their present house is more than enough room. She still claims it's not enough space for their family. It doesn't matter that twenty years ago, a Black man could not have purchased a house in the area they are presently living. It doesn't matter that he is making in one year far and above what most Black men make in two. She's still not satisfied. She considers him to be a piece of shit because the house is "not large enough". Her material standard of value has increased. Accordingly, she pressures her husband to accommodate her new standard. Were he to do so, she would only raise the standard again, and again be unsatisfied. He's *'a nothing'* in her eyes, not because of any flaw in his character, or because he has failed to provide for his family, but because he can't make that unnecessary four to five bedroom upgrade. She's an ungrateful Black woman and he's a fool for attempting to satisfy her. As Black men we can never permit your woman to operate this way. Greed and selfishness must be checked at their very outset. If he were a righteous Black man he'd pack her bags and tell her to go get a five bedroom place by herself or with some other Black man foolish enough to put up with her mess.

Black men also, have to cease and desist from accepting as their *only* standard of value, the materialistic value system or one that places a greater value on things than it does on personal integrity and human life. There are plenty of faggots who have lots of money, but they are faggots just the same. That Black clothing designer, Willie (of Willie's Wear) died rich *and* with AIDS. I'd rather live a modest wholesome and long life, able to see the sunrise each day, than a brief one as an *"AID-ified"* fag, phasing out like a shriveled up string bean. That's no way for a real man to go. Every fag who dies of AIDS has received exactly what he deserved.

As I said, the responsibility for the development of a Black system of values should not rest in the laps of whites. Black value systems should be constructed by Black men who are thinking in terms of what is best for Black people, not what is best for white society. All that is outside the construct of a Black value system designed by, and for Blacks should be seen as worthless. I had one Black man sigh and then say to me *"but you know, the white standard is the only standard I have"*. He felt obliged to function upon it. Fortunately, he's had a chance to visit Africa and have that view mitigated a bit. It's a real tragedy that when the white man proclaims that this or that is now a sign of individual worth, we buy it hook line and sinker. When I say "we", I'm referring to Black men who are ultimately responsible for the moral structure of the race or the lack thereof. TV tells the *"home boys"* that the BMW was a sure sign that a man was a man. Young Black men and women buy that idiotic bill of goods. The *"home boys"* will start selling drugs in order to buy BMW's. It used to be the Cadillac. But whatever it is, it's something that whites came up with for blacks and not the other way around. Men we've got to do a far better job of being inventive, creative, constructive. As I said, we Black men are responsible for the morality of our race. We have to become more involved in the decisions that take place affecting this morality. When TV portrays Black men as overcome with greed, criminals, pompous buffoons, and irresponsible clowns, it reinforces in the minds of Black women that Black men are good for nothing but a laugh. These TV images are impressed into the minds of our women and children all day, every day, each year of their lives. I'll give you one guess as to how a child is going to think about himself or about you by the age of 14, after such exposure. I'll give you one more guess as to what a Black woman is going to think about Black men after such a saturation. But don't misunderstand what I'm saying. These negative images are damaging. That's a fact. Yet there is a serious question to be raised as to whether these images do, or do not, represent the current nature of Black men in America.

We'll be discussing this issue latter on in the book.

4

The American Black woman is a *"time waster"*. She's been wasting *YOUR* time. Were I a white man, I'd gladly prefer *her* as an attack weapon instead of my M-79 or 60 caliber machine gun. I can miss the target with the guns but I *can't* miss with the Black woman. She's deadly. She's accurate. She's infinitely more effective than a Desert Storm high-tech laser weapon. Home her in on any Black man, push the go button and she'll destroy the target. Yes, she's playing a deadly video game and Black men are the target. It's **'Joystick set, aim taken, push the fire button, zoom, splat'!** The Black woman has just taken out another Back man. I've criticized Black men for being the passive targets in the game. The game is called *"Let the White man keep control of Black men"*. It's a game played all over America. The objective of the game is obvious; to control and/or destroy the Black male. White males are slightly ahead so far but don't forget. This book is all about getting *YOU* ahead. They're ahead in large part because **BLACK MEN HAVE BEEN DUMB ENOUGH TO PLAY IT**. On the game screen, you're controlled in many ways, the most effective being the following;

1. **Through your obsession with sports.**
2. **Your obsession with singing and dancing (shuffling).**
3. **Your love of white women.**
4. **Your willingness to waste your time with hostile Black women.**

5

Black men, you've been the perfect passive player. You've been easy to beat. You've done 1 to 4 exceedingly well. While you're watching sports, your woman is reading women's lib literature and telling your daughter to grab a handful of material too. You're no threat to Mr. White Man. You're too occupied with that football point spread. Each Sunday you're at the TV, all day long, while your woman is on the phone with her girlfriends talking a bunch of crap and plotting different ways to undermine what little power and authority you have. Yes gentlemen, while you hide your head in the arena of armchair sports, your Black woman is teaching scum dog, trash, women's liberation ideas to your children. She's teaching by explicit statements or implicitly by her disrespectful, argumentative, unco-operative conduct. Your daughters will turn out to be just as disagreeable as their mother. Your sons will turn out to be weaklings after a life of browbeating from his man hating mom. This generation will, in turn, breed another generation of perverts and weaklings. One Black girl I spoke with began to tell me how the woman's group she belonged to gave her a *"new and enlightened view of reality"*, as she put it. She claimed her experience broadened her horizons and made her more tolerant of others. She began to tell me about the number of lesbian women in the group and how she had come to understand and accept them as a viable minority entitled to the full protection of the civil law. She was fully in favor of gay rights. She continued to *"explain"* to me that gays were gay not by choice but they were born that way and that we had to accept them as another one of God's beloved. She had her two children right there with her, about the ages of five and seven. Her husband had been part of the conversation, but had gone off to watch TV. I didn't believe this was happening. Men, right is right and wrong is wrong. You can try to BS your way around either, but when you're done, right remains right and wrong remains wrong. It was a shame that the husband walked off knowing what she was saying, and let her continue this talk in front of the children. He abrogated his responsibility to insure that the moral tone of the home was wholesome. The two children, both boys, are going to be raised by a woman who takes an active position in support of homosexuality while her husband takes the passive position of acquiescence to madness. I'm led to think of that passage in Scripture which talks about those who turn truth of God into a lie. The truth of God stands against homosexuality.[8] During these very formative and critical years of their lives, the children will have impressed on their brains a total perversion of truth. They'll be raised to believe that which is bad is good, and that which is good is bad. Living in America where it's already hard enough for a strong Black man to survive, this Black mother will have raised her children in a manner which insures their weakness and their defeat at the hands of their enemies. Such perverse and degenerate training will have occurred also because their Black father committed the sin of acquiescence in the face of immorality. Gentlemen, that father should have put a halt to this woman's madness. At the very least he should have told her that if she felt compelled to think that way, she was to keep it to herself. She was not to teach the children that trash. That woman is a perfect example of a degenerate piece of filth. She hears the white man talk mess and buys it hook line and sinker. That Black man is another perfect example of a disgrace. He allows his woman to infect his children with trash ideas. Women are weak. They rarely have an individual thought. They're not capable of rigorous analytical thinking because they are governed by their emotions. A casual inspection of the women's lib platform and today's liberal and egalitarian notions reveals the utter absurdity of their concepts. Yet Black women have bought this foolishness without putting it through rigorous analysis. Had they done so, they might have seen the fallacy of the ideas. They've bought the white man's trash at the price of their children's character. Whatever the white man puts forth as ideal, the Black woman will pass on to their children as gospel truth. Donahue says we should accept with open arms, homosexuals infected with AIDS. Because he says it, many people hold it as gospel. Black women buy that mess because they're mentally weak. Black men permit their weakness to go unchecked. As Black men, we should refuse to accommodate the sensibilities of the Phil Donahues of the world, that is the weak and perverted. Call a spade a spade. Call a fag a fag and don't be squeamish about it. Take a stand and reject what is not true and don't be afraid to be this resolute. Why do you allow yourselves to be silent when you know what is being said and what is happening is untrue and ruinous to yourself and your children. I am incensed that the man I just spoke of let his wife preach the things she did. Who's woman is she? She's not *his*. She's Donahue's.

Black men, teach your sons to be men. Don't let them

grow up believing that fags have a civil right to screw another man in the butt. Stop letting pro fag, pro feminist Phil Donahue talk you into accepting perverts and perverse ideas as normal and acceptable. Stop letting Donahue make you feel guilty for disliking fags and these new independent women. Stop thinking that because a particular conduct may be *frequent* conduct, it must therefore be *acceptable* conduct. Murder occurs frequently, but is it acceptable? I can't stand it when a fag lover and women's libber says to me,

> "How in the world can you preach discrimination against the gay community. You should know better. You're Black and the victim of discrimination. You should join hands with all people who are discriminated against so we can put an end to it. Blacks, women, gays, why we're all part of the oppressed minority."

To begin with, I let them know that the problem of discrimination against me because I'm Black is *my* problem and *I'll* have to work on it. The fags will have to work on their own problem. I have no obligation to help them with what is their unique problem, namely insuring the conditions necessary to screw another man's rear without the sanctions of society at large. Why I'm an old fag basher from way back. I don't want to change in mid-stream. I've every right to like and dislike whatever I wish. There is absolutely no basis for assuming that because I'm discriminated against, I must automatically identify with anybody else who is discriminated against. If there were a KKK family living in my neighborhood who were suffering the discrimination of the surrounding Black community, I'd feel no obligation at all to join forces with the KKK family merely because they're discriminated against and in the general society, so am I. We have to stop falling for that sort of trash logic. It's a sign of mental weakness when you succumb to this nonsense way of thinking. Take care of your own. Take care of *your* tribe. If those outside your tribe have a problem, let them handle their own mess just like we Black men have to handle our own mess. Right now in history, our

8   KJV; Rom. 1:24-32

biggest mess is that American Black woman we've been dealing with. You Black men had better leave women's rights alone, gay rights alone, the rights of the whales and snail darters, and focus in on Black men's rights. It's these rights that are slipping away. When these are utterly gone, the fact that gay's are free, or PMS woman are running the show, or animals have sanctuaries, won't do a darn thing for you. Everybody will have some rights accept you. You'll be in the shit pit where all weak, lackluster, inattentive, perverts should be. But don't worry, we'll appeal to all the liberated women, lesbians and fags to leave a few basketballs in the pit for you to play with. That's been keeping you happy in life so far, no reason to think it won't continue to be enough. Buy the way, while you're down there, think about whether you look respectful from up here. What do you think?

6

> *Who can find a virtuous woman ? for her price is far above rubies.*
>
> *The heart of her husband doth safely trust in her, so that he shall no need of spoil.*
>
> *She looketh well to the ways of her household , and eatethnot the bread of idleness.*

Mr. Black man you're a real good dancer too. The whole world knows you can't out perform you when it comes to snazzy foot shuffling. When I was in Rome, we went to a night club and as soon as we walked in, all eyes turned to us. The disc jockey took off the Italian music and began to play an Italian version of American disco music. *"Ah lub Amer-dee-ka"* the song went. The Italians backed off the stage to see how we were going to dance. After we began, they came back on stage and tried to emulate us. We're good, real good. The whole world recognizes our outstanding contribution to modern day humanity; foot shuffling, hoop throwing, and joke telling. While you and your "home boys" are practicing the latest dance steps, your girlfriends are grouping together and telling each other that you aren't shit. They're saying that all you're good for is a quick hump each night and maintaining the beat on the dance floor. You're no threat to white society. You're too occupied with the *"electric slide"* and the *"moon walk"*. Don't let me give you a false impression. Sinbad makes me laugh so hard I get stomach aches. I love watching the man. I get a kick watching, every once in a while, Soul Train dancers. I'm not begrudging Magic Johnson for being good at what he does. I'm only saying that we as Black men have got to stop believing that we can *ONLY* excel in these areas.

   I have discussed with several friends of mine the significance of entertainment in America as it relates to Black people. I find myself in a difficult position in these discussions. They argue that the only avenues to prosperity open for a Black man in America is sports, singing, dancing, and crime. To them, this is a clear and simple truth. I can't argue with the fact that in general these avenues *ARE* the avenues blacks are taking as their road to prosperity. I do however argue with the assumption that it's etched in stone that sports, entertainment, and crime are now, and forever, the only roads a Black man can take to prosperity. Again, the historical record is clear. No nation of peoples have ever risen to power and prosperity through sports and entertainment. An interesting aspect of our discussions concerns the issue of a nation's rise to prosperity and its participation in criminal activity. It is not altogether unreasonable to propose that America rose to greatness as a result of crime. The early settlers were exiled European criminals. In addition, the early Americans committed genocide against the native peoples. You might argue then, that criminals, committed mass murder and the result was a great nation. As a matter of fact the country of Australia was a European penal colony. The British Caribbean islands were also used to absorb European criminals and rebels. The isle of Barbados was used as a dumping grounds for Scottish exiles who were convicted of felonies or who were banished because of acts their participation in acts of sedition and rebellion. Detailed lists of these persons was kept indicating their crime, the number of persons accompanying them and where they were to be exiled.[9] There is no precedent in history for a race of people becoming affluent through sports, entertainment, or politics I might add. However there is precedent for a race of people becoming not only affluent, but powerful as a result of what can be argued as criminal conduct. I can not honestly say one way or another whether Black men in America will build their "Nation" by being criminals, or as a result of criminal activity in this same context the Europeans built America. I'll wait and see what course we take.

I would like to think that one day our people will rise to a position of affluence and power and not be merely a race of entertainers and buffoons. I'd like to think that one day they will cease to be the non creative players at the brunt end of a consumer society, producing nothing, contributing nothing, just going round and round in cycle of working for whites and giving them the hard earned wages right back. I'd like to think that as a race of people we can be a bit more accomplished than that. Certainly, to the extent that our creative energies are confined to fancy footwork on the dance floor, fancy spins on the way up for the slam dunk, and hitting the high note at the mike, they are not being spent trying to structure a Black economic system that works out for our benefit and relieves us from being at the mercy of white philanthropy, last hired first fired. You know the deal. But it's the only deal you've got because it's the only deal you've bothered to take (I would have preferred to use the word 'negotiate' rather than 'take' but you didn't negotiate your status at all, you accepted it lock stock and barrel). Don't worry though Mr. White man, my home

---

[9]   As an example of such records, see **"The Original List of Persons of Quality and Others..."**, John Camden Hotten, 1874, which list the exiles from Scotland and England to the British Isles, including the name of the ship they travel on, the date of departure, and the number of persons they travelled with and those person's relationship to the primary exile. This particular book I was compelled to use when I was doing my family's genealogical research

.boys won't be an economic threat to you. They're too occupied right now at "the mix". The music sure sounds good. *Chez Whitte's Shuffle Lounge* is open Mr. Black. Hop on in. The cover charge is only $10.00. Sorry I can't join you. I've got a few other things to do.

7

Some of you think that heaven is a night in a white girls arms. Give one of these Black men a white woman and he'll scrape his finger tips doing cartwheels praising the lord for this marvelous gift. Why to him "white stuff" is the *only* stuff. But let me stop being be so mean. After all, the Black stuff is so disagreeable and cruel, so raunchy and over used, what's a fellow going to do? It's common among the Black bourgeois to think that their rise to an Affirmative Action, Set Aside, middle management position must be crowned with a white wife. Mr. Black is quiet now, cool and happy. Mr. Gringo can retire him from the active duty list of Black men likely to resist oppression. But I want to make it clear that I understand these men are dammed if they do, and dammed they don't. I guess they figure that they'll draw criticism for choosing the white girl but they'll draw the pangs of hell for choosing an American Black girl. On balance they calculate it better they go the white route. Perhaps this is courage. I leave it to the reader to decide. I have to admit, as a parent, I don't want my children exposed to constant battles in the home. I'd be hard pressed to make a decision if my only choices were an obnoxious, degenerate American Black woman or a white women who would give me respect. It's hard for me to argue against a man who has taken the white route, if I enter his home and see he's being treated well, and that they both are happy. My arguments against what he's done become, at that point, purely political or philosophical in nature. I can't argue against it on practical grounds because *"the thing is workin"*. I do have a problem with Black men who take on the white girl as the final expression of success in America. Such a motivation, does not a good marriage make.

8

Finally, we have the ultimate weapon, the American Black woman, sassy as she wants to be, a disgraceful D.O.B. and the ultimate time waster. Perhaps you had great plans for yourself in life. You're discovering that you can't find the time and energy to implement them. Your time is spent arguing with some ignorant American Black woman about things you know to be true and things she obviously has no knowledge of at all. You know that you'll fall into a mud hole if you turn left. She knows it too, but just because *YOU* had the nerve to say don't turn left, she feels compelled to do the exact opposite. She'll argue, turn left, then fall in the mud hole. If you were white, she would have obeyed your directive. The real tragedy is *not* that by failing to obey you she falls in the pit, good riddance, but that *you're taking your precious time arguing with her.* Look gentlemen, if the bitch wants to sink let her! Believe me, it'll be a load off your shoulders. You'll get a lot more accomplished in life without her. Besides, these American Black women get mighty loud when they start opening their mouths and arguing. You stand an excellent chance of damaging your ear drums. It's like noise pollution. That's exactly what the American Black woman is doing with that mouth of hers, creating noise pollution. As a matter of fact, all she is at this point in history is one gigantic piece of noise pollution. Yes, you're a good player in the game Mr. Black man. This American Black woman is taking up all your time being ridiculous. By the time you get to the battlefield, ready to fight the white man, you've no more energy. You're all tuckered out after arguing with that American Black woman. You're no threat. You're too tired to fight. Mr. Black, you're a real good boy now, You're under control.

CHAPTER-THREE

Chocolate Thunder
or
Chocolate Blunder
Is She Making war, not Love?

1

Mr. Black man, you're getting hit from all sides. There's no peace. You walk outside your house every day and *the man* tries to bust you down. You enter your castle and your woman continues where the man left off. You need relief and Alka Seltzer isn't good enough. Well, let's go over again what you're going through.

Men and women approach the world through different perspectives. They see the same life phenomena but analyze it and respond to it totally differently. For thousands of years this has been true. For thousands of years women have caused men problems. The scriptures talk about the contentious woman causing a man problems. Thousands of years ago women were a pain in the rear and they continue to be a pain in the rear today. Their fundamental nature is a problem for us, but for a disciplined man, it's a manageable problem. Men have managed the problem of a woman's negative nature primarily by being strong and inflexible. Historically, men have maintained a rigid standard of permissible conduct to which women were obliged to conform. Failing conformity, she was punished. Her punishment was swift and certain. Proverbs caution us;

"Lust not after her beauty in thine heart; neither let her take thee with her eyelids. For by means of a whorish woman, a man is brought to a piece of bread. Can a man take a fire in his bosom, and his clothes not be burned?".[10]

10   KJV Ps 6:26

When I read that, I laughed and said, Lord the *last* thing you have to worry about when it comes to me, is falling for some American Black woman's eyelids. She ain't leading me anywhere. I'll get my slice of bread from somewhere else. The angels don't want that beast, why should I mess with her. Later I read,

> "It is better to dwell in the wilderness, than with a contentious and angry woman".[11]

Well gentlemen, you can bet your last nickel that it'll snow in the Sahara desert before I let myself live in the wilderness because of some evil American Black woman. However, I've no problem with sending her there. I'm a double standard man and proud of it.

2

At this point in time, I don't believe the American Black woman's nature will change for the better. Those few who are squared away will remain so. The majority of these air heads will remain as such. Scripture says,

> "He that is unjust, let him be unjust still; and he which is filthy, let him be filthy still; and he that is righteous, let him be righteous still..."[12]

I think you waste your time by trying to change the unchangeable. I believe the American Black woman is basically unchangeable at this point in history. Scriptures make it clear, that there comes a time when nothing else can be done. It's like a play that has been written and Act One has been performed. When Act One is over, it doesn't matter how good or bad it was because you can't go back and re-do it, at least not at that performance. The audience is waiting to see the rest of the play. You have to move on to the next act and do a better job with Act One during tomorrow night's show. With respect to the current

---
11   KJV Bible, Ps 21:9
12   KJV Bible, Rev. 21:11

status of Black male-female relationships, I'm going to argue latter on that Act One got screwed up. I'm going to argue that we have to forget Act One and go on with the rest of the play of life's struggles. We'll get a chance to improve our performance with the next day's performance. I'll explain what I mean by this latter on in the book.

So, gentlemen, I think when it comes to the nature of women, you can't alter her negative characteristics. All you can do is mitigate them with constraints upon her, designed to dampen her negative side somewhat. In other words, you prevent the full expression of her negativity from disturbing your inner peace, or 'wa' as the Japanese would say. With your constraints, only a minor portion of her negative nature will break the surface. To sum it up, let me call the fundamental contentious nature of a woman, **Characteristic-#1**.

American men, white or Black, in addition to having to deal with characteristic-#1, must deal with that part of a woman's character which results from her absorption of society's values. To the extent that the overall values of the society are wholesome, she will tend to be wholesome. To the extent that the overall values of society are perverse, she will tend to be a pervert (Remember, women are reactionary. Their conduct and ideals are always and only a function of what men make available to them. They will never create a new way of thinking and doing things. At best they will try to mirror the conduct of men. This is what the practical result of the Women's movement accomplished, women trying to act like men). American society is perverse. It's predicated on greed and an indifference to the plight of ones fellow man. Americans revel in greed. They are amongst the greediest people on Earth. In the late 70's, Ex-President Jimmy Carter said *"The dominant philosophy in America today is greed"*. Corruption abounds in the highest levels of government down to the street corner. Capitalism teaches greed, selfishness and indifference. All this is perverse. This perversion adversely affects men and women. The average American woman is not only a pain in the behind because she is a woman, but also because her nature is further aggravated by the extreme and excessive greed dominant in American Society. I'm going to call this greed **Characteristic**

#2. Women's greed is insatiable. You men out there know that if you give them one nice perhaps expensive trinket, they're not satisfied until they get the ultimate trinket, and even then they're still not satisfied. I had a friend of mine remark that if you trace the roots of crime in America it lies in men's attempts to satisfy a woman's greed. The man has to make himself look prosperous in the eyes of the woman. The more material objects he displays and gives, the more a woman is likely to give him attention. If he can't get hold of material things through ordinary work, he'll commit crimes, all to satisfy the greed of a woman.

Black men have to contend with characteristics #1 and #2 plus the component of a Black woman's hostility and overall bad attitude. I'm going to call this **Characteristicá#3**. If we charted this out it would look like:

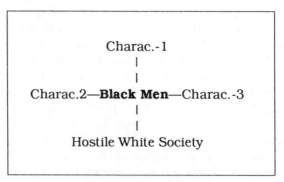

```
                Charac.-1
                    |
                    |
   Charac.2—Black Men—Charac.-3
                    |
                    |
           Hostile White Society
```

All men have to deal with at least one negative aspect of a woman's nature. American men, Black and white have to deal with two negative aspects of a woman. The first is an inevitable consequence of her being a woman. The second is socially induced, that is it's a result of how a society conditions its woman to be. Sometimes the effect of Characteristic-#2 is *'no effect at all'* or I should say, *'no negative effect at all'*. At other times it's a catastrophic effect as in the case of the encouragements of the women's libers who would have every woman in the world rebel against men. Black American men have to deal with four negative aspects. The first two, plus the added component of a Black woman's hostility. The Black must also combat the general hostility of white society at large. He's fighting on four fronts. We could diagram it like this;

```
What ALL men deal with
    Characteristic-1 +
    Characteristic-2 +


What Black Men deal with
    Characteristic-1 +
    Characteristic-2 +
    Characteristic-3 +
    Hostile American Society
```

Black men, give yourself some credit. You've been totally surrounded but you're still hanging on. Your position is not as strong as it could be but you're still in there. You've the makings of a real warrior. White men could never stand up to the pressure you've had to endure. They don't have the sort of courage it takes. They commit suicide at the drop of a hat. They would long ago have decimated their numbers this way. You're strong. You're just not mentally organized. You're walking around with erroneous and conflicting thoughts about a lot of different things. These thoughts imputed to you by white society. You need to get rid of these thoughts. I'm going to help you define them and rid yourself of them. They're not your thoughts. They won't work in your best interest. You need to develop your own set of beliefs. You need to be more effective planners and strategist. You need an offensive strategy. You've been able to stave off total annihilation, but this is a defensive approach. It's not sufficient to merely stave off attacks. You must also be creative and constructive. You must create the conditions that utterly discourage and preclude attacks or sabotage from your enemies. You must make a potential enemy less likely to move against you for fear of either your massive retaliation, or because he knows that tactically, his attack will fail. This was the U.S. policy towards the Soviet Union. The Soviets were discouraged from attacking because of the possibility of a U.S. retaliation so devastating that even if the Soviets "won" in a nuclear exchange, the figured that their own land would have been torn to pieces by U.S. nuclear counter strikes. In such an instance, the price of Soviet victory would be too high.

Gentlemen, you have to have an offensive strategy as I just said. You also have to have a defensive policy which is tantamount to a *"Dooms Day Machine"*. Your enemies have to know that even if they wipe you out, you'll bring them down from the grave. Your vengeance must be that thorough As I said, you can't win battles if all of your energies are spent on the defensive. Right now Black men, you're on the defensive. You've been on the defensive for the past few decades. You can't hold out this way forever. White males have been in a conspiracy with Black women, against you. They've both been on the offense. I'm not necessarily suggesting that Black women are consciously aware that they are part of the conspiracy. In many instances they're being used unawares. The sad thing is that when most of them realize that they're being used, they don't care. They transform from unwitting allies of white males, to willing co-conspirators against the interest of Black men. I once heard a sales girl say she read Shahrazad Ali's book.[13] I asked her if she agreed with what Ms. Ali was saying. She said "yes". I then asked her if she thought she was guilty of being the sort of woman Ms. Ali criticized. She responded "yes". I asked her if she thought being this way was terrible. She again replied "yes". I then asked her if all of these realizations motivated her to make a change in her ways she said "No! I am this way. I've been this way for a long time and I'll continue to be this way". She became a willing partner of the white man.

If left unchecked, the tactics of white males and their lackeys, the American Black woman, will prevail over your passivity. They will gradually chip away at you until you're less than dirt, or dead. Gentlemen, this hour is a critical one for Black men in America. We've got to rally and kick ass. We have to consolidate our forces and hit the strategy conference tables again. We're being moved on and we're not counter attacking.

[13] The Blackman's Guide to Understanding the Black Woman, Shahrazad Ali' 1989

Women have been active. We have been passive. I've heard Black men say *"aw the best way to deal with her shit is to just ignore it. I just go out and play ball with the boys or something"* Gentlemen, **THIS WILL NOT DO**. What do you think your son is thinking when he sees you responding to your disrespectful Black woman by running away and putting your head in the sand. What message do you think you're sending to that Black woman? Your passive response reinforces, in her mind, a belief that you're a faggot, a weak and worthless chump except for a shot at night. One girl I knew told me that most Black women are taught by their mothers from the age of four years old that "Black men ain't shit". I asked several other Black women about this and they each told me they were taught similarly by their mothers in more or less the same words. They're taught that Black men are shiftless and have no guts and that they can't face a problem square in the face and lick it. When you use the "I'll ignore her" approach, you confirm this view in the minds of Black woman.

Our passivity in the face of women's activity has placed us in a very weak position. Our passivity has encouraged Black women to become more and more negative, and to have less and less respect for us. But let's be honest, Black men. Why should Black women respect us. There really aren't any adverse consequences to them when they don't. If there were, they wouldn't be the way they are. We have given license to them to be real bitches. Right now, they're so bad, I believe most of them are damaged beyond repair. They can't be rehabilitated. They're like rotten apples that can't be made good. I believe the next three to five years will be critical for Black men in America. During this time, Black men must begin to stand up to their women and put them in their place. *"Her place"* just might have to be some place other than with you. If you have an extraordinary woman she might see the light and correct her evil ways. I believe the majority however, are so infested with hostility towards Black men, so infested with the disease of the American perverse, capitalistic value system, that they will never make a change. We'll know in a few years. I know a few men who are faced with some rather contentious Black woman. They feel they can turn that woman around. I wish them luck. If they can't they have to begin to think of alternatives. There are millions of African women dying for the chance to make you a decent, gentle, considerate and humble wife. There are millions of Asian and Latin American women willing to do the same. I know several Black men who have already taken this step, myself included. They are currently developing relationships with African and Asian women and report life as blissful compared to life with this raunchy American Black girl. If the American Black woman can't change herself, then you'll have to change her. By that I don't mean trying to rehabilitate her. I mean you have to unplug her from the circuit board of your life and replace her with someone who is going to be co-operative, dutiful, respectful and useful. Remember what I said earlier. Black Women of America aren't the only women in the world. Let me repeat that. **BLACK WOMEN OF AMERICA ARE NOT THE ONLY WOMEN IN THE WORLD!** You'll be surprised to discover how easy it is to make contact with a foreign woman and establish a rapport with her. You'll be astonished at the difference in her attitudes as compared to these corrupt and degenerate American Black girls. Men, you have to stop pussy footing around. You have to be bold. You have to take a stand. You have to make a move. Stop all your complaining about these women and just replace them. All the complaining in the world won't change them. They're too evil. Dark & Lovely? Bull! Black and miserable. That's what they are.

You have to stop trying to BS yourself. Stop playing head games with yourself. Stop trying to call an apple a pear. Call a spade a spade. These women are degenerate. Be a man and admit it. I had one young Black man say to me "but American Black women are the finest looking women in the world". My response was a quick "So What!". I like looking at them too. I think they are among the most attractive women on the planet, but so what! If I want to look at them, they're there. If you want to screw a few of them, just give them a few dollars they'll jump. But you don't take them into your home as wives. They are not wife material, not the American ones. They're good for a look and a screw but not for wives. They have not proven themselves to be fit for such a holy enterprise. You want a decent, agreeable Black woman? Look to Africa. Look to Asia. Look to Latin America and the Caribbean. But whatever you do, leave these hands on hip, spear chukkers alone. Too bad we can't lobby congress to pass a bill giving each negative American Black woman a plastic spear and sending her to the Congo to fight lions. She loves combat. Let her go at it in the jungle where she belongs. The plastic spear is symbolic of her worth. She's disposable. Dispose of her! The U.S. House of Representatives could have called the bill **HR 51-GET-BACK**. The senate version could have been called **S 74-REGRET-NEGRESS.**

Gentlemen, I've vivid recollections of visiting a friend of mine in 1977 who married a lady from the Philippines. His wife brought me out a glass of Pepsi. He and I were engrossed in our conversation. After about a half an hour it occurred to me that *"something wasn't right here"*. I knew I had been drinking that soda the entire time I was sitting at the kitchen table but my glass was still full. Was I in the twilight zone? The answer was yes! I was in the twilight zone of true hospitality. What was *"wrong"* was me not being used to good treatment. It turns out that the entire time I was talking to my friend, his wife had been monitoring me and re-filling my glass. She had been doing it without me even knowing it was happening. I mentioned this to my friend who just laughed and said *"When you're in our home you can forget all that negative treatment you get from those Black girls. It's a different ball game here.."* He was correct. A Black woman would never have been so hospitable. It takes all her strength to get up even the tiniest bit of energy to attend to her own man's needs, let alone a visitor. The Black women would have felt hard pressed to get you a half glass of water and if she did, you were on your own after that. I know that the women who are reading this right now are so mad, they're about to vomit. The concept of serving your man and his guest is probably as repulsive to them as their obnoxiousness is to most of you. Men, let that Black woman wallow in the filth of her own bad attitudes. You move on to better things. Look to Africa. Look to Asia. Look to Latin America and the Caribbean. There's gold in them there hills. These American hills have nothing but sand and it's all lumpy with seagull dung.

When we get to discussing options, I'll pass on to you. some information about establishing contact with ladies from other countries.

CHAPTER-FOUR
Are my shoes shined?

Gentlemen, I say to people all the time *"don't call my shoes muddy unless yours are shinned"*. It's within this context I write this chapter. What I'm about to say is going to sting your butts. Believe me, it stings me too. I've still got a few edges I have to get squared away in my own life. Until I accomplish this, I can't complain about some of the flack I may get for being "dirty".

What I am about to say is said **NOT** in a spirit of condemnation but that of constructive criticism. It hurts me to see so many Black men going through so much aggravation with their women. I think it's tragic that our ego's have been a stumbling block. Our ego's have prevented us from rallying together, admitting our failings and correcting them. A real macho man is oblivious to pain. Right now, I'm talking about emotional pain. As Black men, we have to soldier. Soldiering includes the ability to go through the pain of justified criticism.

Black men, there's a very simple truth we have to face up to. It's hard to face it. It's painful. I squirm each time I have to say this. Gentlemen, the plain fact is that in America today, we aren't shit. We get no respect. White America doesn't respect us. Our own women don't respect us either. Half our kids think we aren't worth the dirt in our socks. We're catching hell because we get no respect. It's *"crap on the Black man"* time in America and it's so easy to do. We get crapped on each way we turn. We get crapped on when we turn to the left. We get crapped on when we turn to the right. Look up, or look down, we're getting crapped on. It's 1992 and it's still open season on the Black man. Come one, come all, let's crap on a Black. It's fun. We're getting crapped on men because we're *"crappable"*, if I may be so bold as to make up a word. We've been passive. We've just let everybody come along and take giant shits, on us. Everybody feels free to do as they please to

53

the Black man. They feel certain there are no repercussions from him.

Where I live, there are hundreds of Korean shops selling all sorts of things at exorbitant prices. I hear Black men complain about the Koreans every day. I hear them talking about the Koreans *"taking over"*. In Philadelphia and New York, you get the feeling that a Korean store owner will shoot a Black person if you so much as stare too hard at a bag of potato chips. They get away with it. Why? Because the Koreans know that Black men are passive. We won't do a darn thing if they crap on us. We're passive and they're active. In Philly a Korean shot a Black person and surprisingly the neighborhood got up enough gumption to boycott the store. Along comes a weak chump of a school teacher, Black as he wants to be. He brought along some of his students to break the boycott. He crossed the neighborhood picket lines and entered the Korean store with the kids to show support for the Koreans. The Negro even bought a few items. News media had a field day with the story. They played him like a hero. You'd better believe though, in the privacy of the news room, the whities were saying,

> *"I just don't believe these niggers. They're dumb as all hell. How could this boy support the same people who just shot two of them without even flinching?"*

News media continued the story. Ahhh, Mr. Black hero, pride of the white man, striking a blow for fairness to the Koreans. Mr. Black Hero was striking a blow for Korean Freedom. Well the media discovered that this teacher had a prior conviction for drugs and had not advised the school board. When this hit the fan, he was fired from his job. Do you think the Koreans came along and supported the man? Do you think they offered him employment or anything at all. No! I can hear them telling this dumb Black *"Aw too bad you got fired. Thanks for the support you've shown us dummy. Se ya latter"*. He was just another dumb nigger who got crapped on. But why did he get crapped on? **BECAUSE HE ALLOWED IT TO HAPPEN. HE INVITED IT.** He might as well stayed at home that day, called up everybody in the universe and said *"Hey yawl, here I is. Please take a giant crap on my face. I ain't worth nuttin!"*. What sort of role model is this man to Black children? How much respect does he command from Black women. How much respect would you give him?

Let's take a look at the one incident which best demonstrates the degree to which back men don't get respect, The infamous **WILSON GOODE BOMB OUT.** For those few of you who may not know what I'm talking about, I'm referring to he bombing from the air of a house in a West Philadelphia Black neighborhood by a police helicopter. The bombing started a fire which eventually destroyed a whole square block of homes. Mr. Black Mayor, The **'Honorable'** Wilson Goode will go down in history as the ultimate disgrace. Those of you who followed hearings of the commission charted to investigate the bombing were probably as shocked and disgusted as I was when we heard the gory details of that day. The police dropped a bomb on a hose occupied by members of an organization called **MOVE.** A fire resulted and began to spread to adjoining homes. Goode gave the on scene fire commissioner orders to put the fire out. The on scene police commissioner with full knowledge of Goode's orders, countermanded them and ordered that the Fire Department Commissioner let the fire continue to burn. By the time the police commissioner 'consented' to putting out the fire, it was too late. An entire neighborhood went up in flames and eleven people died including five children. What is significant is that the white police commissioner ignored and/or countermanded the orders of his commander in chief, Mr. Black Man Mayor, The Honorable Wilson Goode. You see, gentlemen, the police commissioner had no fear of Goode, no respect for him. To him Goode was just a nigger with a title but a nigger just the same. I watched Goode on several occasions presenting a belligerent and authoritative posture with respect to Black people while at other times, in front of an audience of whites, he would present what was to me, a conciliatory and meek tone. As far as I'm concerned, Goode was a perfect example of weakness. The police commissioner must have considered him as such. He would never dared to ignore the orders of a superior if he thought that superior would kick his ass. When Goode became aware that his orders were not being obeyed he should have been right on the scene and fired that commissioner. He should have gone down the chain of command if necessary, firing every individual on the spot until his orders were obeyed. He was just too weak to do it. The end result was that a neighborhood was destroyed and lives of children were lost. One neighborhood woman interviewed in front of the smoldering buildings was asked what she had learned from this incident. She remarked that she learned never should one surrender his power and authority to others in order to get a job done that you should do yourself. She had a strong argument. There had been conflict between the neighborhood and the MOVE organization. The MOVE people were among the filthiest people you can imagine. Their filth was the cause of an incredible rat and roach infestation in the area. Their daily bull horn blasting was deafening to the ears. The neighborhood called in the white man and the white man's black lackeys to put an end to it. The white man put an end to MOVE and also to the neighborhood with their bomb by helicopter experiment. This bombing goes down as the first time in the history of America that a city was bombed from the air using a motorized aircraft.[14] The Russians didn't do it. The weakness of Goode did it. Mr. Black Mayor, bombed some Blacks. Grin white man, grin. The truly sad thing is that on the very block the MOVE house was situated, you had military vets. These VETS should have gotten themselves together, marched up on the MOVE place and given them an ultimatum together with a statement of clarity. They should have made it clear that one of two courses of action were certain to follow. Either MOVE would vacate the premises or MOVE members would all be found in the park with broken limbs. Rather than take the bull by the horns, the men of the neighborhood hid behind the skirts of officialdom. Officialdom wound up destroying their neighborhood. I wonder how many men of the area learned the lesson that woman I referred to learned. You can sum the whole thing up like this.

[14] There was an attempt during World War II by some Japanese women. The plan called for tying bombs to balloons and air lifting them to the U.S. coast. The effort was a dismal failure. No bombs ever hit the coast.

The men of the neighborhood failed in their responsibility as men and warriors by handing a problem they should have dealt with themselves, over to the white man and his lackeys. The white man and his lackeys destroyed the entire neighborhood. General George Patton once wrote,

> *"...What manner of man is it who when insulted, hires another to shoulder his responsibility? Even the despised jackal protects its young personally and not through the interposition of some more courageous animal hired by the offer of some choice bit of carrion."* [15]

What do you think our women say to themselves and their girlfriends when they see we'll let them get killed and do nothing about it? Think about that! If you were in their shoes, would you feel secure and protected? What do you think our women are saying each time they give us a hard time and our only reaction is to run to the basketball court? Can our women and children count on us? Can they respect us? I'm not too sure we can expect them to. If as Black men, our shoes aren't shinny, we're on shaky grounds calling a Black woman's shoes muddy.

Julius Caesar commented on the Gallic tribes he had to fight. The Gauls were a tough people. On more than one occasion Caesar's troops mutinied when they knew they had to face some of these Gallic tribes in battle. The Gauls refused to readily submit to oppression. They fought. Each man knew that if he failed to fight he would loose the respect of his own people, of his women. He knew he couldn't allow his women and children to be abused by the Romans without putting up a stiff fight. Just think of it gentlemen, these men over two thousand years ago knew very well what we seem to have forgotten today. If you want to be respected, you must be respectable.

A 19th century French writer named Frederic Bastiat wrote a pamphlet on the nature of Law. In it he said,

---

[15] From a manuscript by George Patton titled War As She Is, Chapter I, The Soldier, 1919

"The safest way to make laws respected is to make them respectable". [16]

Gentlemen, we are supposed to be the law in our homes. Let me expand Bastiat's principle. In order for Black men to be respected, they must be respectable. **ARE WE RESPECTABLE?** Somewhere around 50 B.C., Julius Caesar wrote about his military campaigns against the war-like tribes of the Gauls and Germans. In describing them he said,

"...for each man refuses to allow his own folk to be oppressed and defrauded, since otherwise he has no authority among them"

In the old days, women would come to the battlefield, man the ramparts or the hills and observe their men fighting. Men fought fiercely so as not to be called cowards by their women. They got respect. They were warriors. Now, in our time, a Black man will do anything to avoid protecting his family and fighting his true enemies. We're afraid to fight. Rather than fight the real enemy we'll fight and kill each other. This is a coward's way! We'll allow the enemy to defraud our women and turn them against us. Because of this, our women don't find us respectable. Don't misunderstand me. I'm not putting the blame entirely on you. I'm convinced that even if we were respectable, Black women would still not give us respect. I believe they're too far gone, too brain washed, too evil. Too many of them are a lost cause.

In the opening of Caesar's Gallic Wars, he writes;

"...the Belgae are the most courageous, because they are farthest removed from the culture and the civilization of the Province, and least often visited by merchants introducing the commodities that make for effeminacy;..." [19]

[16] THE LAW, Frederic Bastiat, translation by Dean Russell 1981 @ p.12
[17] THE GALLIC WARS, Julius Caesar, Translation by H.J. Edwards @p333
[18] Meaning the Roman province of Gallia Narbonensis which was established about 121 B.C.
[19] THE GALLIC WARS, Julius Caesar, translation by H.J. Edwards at page 3

Think about that passage with me for a minute. The Gauls were hard pressed by their enemies, the Romans. They knew they had to keep themselves strong at all times. They lived in forest type environment. They couldn't go to the supermarket for food. They had to get off their rear ends and hunt for food. Their women didn't have washers and dryers. Everything was done by hand. They couldn't go get a mortgage for a house or call the local plumber to fix the pipes. Everything they had, everything they lived in, they built with their own hands. Hard work, sweat and tears. This was the sort of thing these people were made of. They knew that if they allowed their society to be infested with luxury items, they would become weak. They would lose their will to resist their enemies. Caesar defines such a transition from strength to weakness as taking on more of an effeminate nature, that is, moving from a masculine nature to a more feminine nature in the sense that men are strong and tackle problems. Women are weak and see their problem situations though rose colored glasses. We have begun to approach our problems in an effeminate manner. That is, we've become weak. We've let the world shit on us without giving any real and consequential resistance. We've let ourselves degenerate into states of apathy and passivity. We've let our women and children go unprotected. We've let them run over to the white man. This is what happens to weak men.

I mentioned to you earlier the calling of that Boston minister in a 1780 sermon. Let me quote him again as he warned what able men ought NOT to be;

"...men that have not broken or debilitated their bodies or minds by the effeminating pleasures of luxury..." [20]

I've seen young black boys standing on the corner with their hands grabbing their crotch.
"Yeah, I'm a bad ass. It's big and well used. I've got more kids out there than Carter has Liver pills"
These boys think they're real macho men. They're full of nonsense. They're nothing more than slimy pieces of shit.

[20]   Simeon Howard, A.M. of Boston Mass, Election Sermon, 1780 as quoted from They Preached Liberty by Franklin P. Cole p.115

Machismo is more than a swinging bird and the ability to punch a girl in the face. Machismo implies a 360o, well rounded, well balanced Black man. A real macho man knows that his dick and his fist are only a minor percentage of his total self. A man with a big bird and callouses on his knuckles, but who catches hell from his woman and is despised by the world, is not a macho man. Where's his sense of macho when Koreans kill his people. Where's his sense of macho when white cops kill Black teenagers with impunity. Where's his sense of macho when his lack of creativity results in his woman begging for food stamps from the white man's welfare system. I'll tell you where his sense of machismo is, *"It isn't is"*, that's where it is. Now that's the long and short of it.

I've spoken of alternatives to the American Black woman. But if you invite a trillion African and Asian ladies here for marriage, you'll solve absolutely nothing if you allow *THEM* to be defrauded and oppressed too. It will do no good if you're going to continue your passive acceptance of abuse from society at large. Men, you have to make a change. There's no getting around this truth. If you don't want to make a change, then you have no right to complain about the treatment you're getting from women.

Aren't you tired of the constant fighting you have to engage in to survive in hostile America? Aren't you tired of having to fight your own household? I know I'd be tired of it. I'd want it to end. Well gentlemen, it'll end when *YOU END IT.* It'll end when you stop being passive and start being creatively active. The whole thing is on your shoulders. You can have what you want. Just make sure that what you want is the best thing to have. You want peace in your household, get yourself mentally organized with some down to earth, hard biting, old fashion truth. Then reconstruct your household. Be creative. If your wife conducts herself as though she were your enemy, and she refuses to change, get rid of her and get one who is willing to treat you with respect. If you have to take more time with yourself contemplating your next strategy, put that basketball down and start contemplating.

CHAPTER-FIVE

Down and Dirty, Semper Fi

1

If you survived the ass kicking you got in Chapter three and you're still hanging in there, you're a real macho man. You've got promise. You're going to make it. Let's get ready for some down to earth strategy and tactics talk. First you have to prime yourself up. You have to get ready for battle. We're going to check our ammo and make sure the radio is working correctly before we move out. By that I mean we've got to get some basic things straightened out first before we can attack with full force, the problem we've been talking about. Let's start. First let's get rid of feminine thinking. We can't afford to give ourselves the *"for the sake of the kids"* argument. That's an excuse. It's what weak women use to justify staying with an extremely abusive man. Get rid of the *"but I love her"* argument too. It's for weaklings. If you can't get rid of these two excuses, you're going to be ineffective. You're going to begin your attack and then do a premature retreat. You'll lose the battle and finally loose the war. You will have shown yourself to be a chump, a weak old faggot, unworthy of anything but contempt from the entire of humanity. So analyze yourself first. Do not continue to read further unless you able to shed any vestige of detrimental feminine thinking. If you don't feel you want to take the candy bars out of your ammo pouch, put this book down now.

Ok, now you're ready to move it out. Have courage! Get primed! What's the spirit of the bayonet? Yeah! Yeah! You're a real Macho man! You're ready! I can feel it. If you've hung in there up to this point, you're hard core. You're ready. We're going to rock this nation. It's going to be like a hurricane has ripped through this land from east coast to west coast, from north to south. We're going to be moving swiftly, turning everything upside down. They won't know what hit them.

When the dust settles, millions of unhappy Black men will be joyous. White society will be defeated and mad as all hell. Millions of time wasting American Black women will be left on the curb. You can't get weak You've been weak for too long. Weakness has gotten you nothing but misery.

You're going to give that American Black woman of yours one last chance. The odds are that she won't make a change but you're going to try and help her. She's the pits. She's funky and low down. She's a real disgrace. Women of this caliber are subhuman. But for the record, you're going to give her one more chance. You're going to tell her outright, that within 24 hours she is to begin a 180o turn about in her attitude, her conduct, and how she treats you. You want her to keep her mouth shut, clean house good, prepare the meal to your satisfaction, control those kids, give out the shot, and smile as she does it. If she's a working woman you don't care. You want these things done anyway. You're willing to lend her a helping hand here and there if you feel like it, but even if you don't, she is still to comply with your new directives. You're going to tell her that you will never again accept that rude tone of voice of hers when she addresses you. You're going to let her know that if she can't control that fat mouth of hers, you'll slap it off her face. You're tired of all her shit. You've had it and it's shape up time or ass kicking time. That, and that alone, is the bottom line. You're going to tell her that you're willing to go a long way with her. You're willing to make a go at a productive relationship, but you won't attempt it unless she changes her ways. You're going to let her know that if she thinks she can do a temporary change just to cool you out 'for a month and then return to her old ways, she's mistaken. You will never accept a regression of her behavior. You are willing at any point in the future, without notice, to sever this relationship.

I want you to stop smiling at her. You smile at your friends and she is not your friend. She must *EARN* the right to be considered your friend. You will keep a straight face at all times. You will never tell her what you are thinking. She must always be wondering and worried about whether you are in a good mood or a bad mood. She ought to be in a constant state of intimidation and fear. Why gentleman if you're doing your job right, when you sneeze, she'll flinch in fear. All this sort of thing is not necessary if you were dealing with a different kind of woman but you're not. You've got that low down negative Black girl. You're in an emergency crises situation which calls for extraordinary emergency measures. It's boot camp, and *YOU* are the *D.I.* You're the man of the hour and she had better not forget it. **"Semper Fi"** gentlemen, **Semper Fi!** She might wind up calling the cops on you or getting a restraining order. *Take it!* She's going to learn that you're not going to allow the system to coerce you into an unconditional acceptance of her foolishness. You understand that this is war and you're prepared to get hit. She's got to learn that the system can't help her. The cops can't help her. Nothing can save her from you, except you. You can even save her from herself if she is able to get through your boot camp. You can't win in war unless you're wiling to accept casualties. And gentlemen I repeat, this *IS* war. If you can't take the incoming rounds, then take all her bull forever. There is no war without casualties.

Remember she's under training, Basic Training. It's like the military. She's entitled to nothing other than a hard time. That's the way it's done in the military. You come into the military full of BS. You've got so much BS. it's coming out your ears. You think you're going to get over with your stuff. But the military has got more tricks in their bag than you have BS. They grab you and tear you down. They break you down to a lump of shit then they rebuild you. You enter a total idiot and you come out righteous. At Fort Jackson they lined us up one day and the D.I. said,

"Some of you will do well in this man's army and some of you will not do well. Those who know the truth will do well. Those who do not know the truth will not do well. What is this truth you're all asking yourself? Well it's simple. It's that you aren't shit. Your mamma's aren't shit. Your Papas aren't shit. Those of you who realize this will do well. Those of you who do not realize this, will not do well."

I was shocked. I didn't believe he was saying this to

ME. But somehow I intuitively knew I had better not argue with the man. Twenty years latter I began to understand what the man was really saying. It was simple. It was that the world has no time for bull. You have to get with the program and do things right or suffer. Gentlemen, this is the basic message you're giving that Black woman of yours. You have no time for her bull. She has to get with your program or suffer.

Gentlemen, you've got to keep the pressure on, keep the training active. You can't let up. You can't waiver in your purpose. She'll be looking for any weakness in you so she can drive a nail right in there. You can' be weak. You've got to be *utterly unfair.* If she comes to you with an idea, nix her. Tell her that you're not interested in her ideas. You have enough ideas for the both of you. Perhaps her idea would have been a good one, but she's under training. She's on probation. She hasn't yet earned the right to have an idea. After all, what have been the quality of her past notions. They've all been about how to disrespect you. Her thoughts are to be seen as fit for only for the garbage pail. I recall a friend of mine who told me he worked in the computer room in Saigon. He's a smart guy and full of ideas. He told his sergeant that there was a more efficient way to run the computer. The sarge looked at him and said,

> "Son, before you, there was OUR way. While you, there is OUR way. After you there will be OUR way. Son, just hop on board and get with the program."

Your woman is less than a PFC. She is a shit head. She hasn't yet graduated from your basic training. Right now there is *YOUR* way and that's the only way that counts. Gentlemen tear her down and rebuild her (if possible). All her trashy, degenerate scum nature must be destroyed and replaced with wholesome attitudes. Remember, *I don't think she can be transformed,* but you know her better than I do. If you think she's worth the effort then that's OK with me! I wish you luck. If she's sitting down relaxing when you enter the room, don't even give her the courtesy of a glance. She's a nothing. She's not yet entitled to recognition. If you should also sit down in the room, make sure your activities are totally unrelated to her.

Make sure that whatever you're doing doesn't include her. She's a non-being until she has proven herself worthy of civilized enterprise. She must be considered subhuman until she proves herself. If she should interrupt you, frown and look mean. Invoke fear in her heart. Black women and Russians are alike. They only understand power. They need to fear. (Why if congress won't send them to the Congo, perhaps we can send them off to Siberia where they can freeze their butts off). By now she should be so scared of you that if she interrupts you, her voice is wavering and timid. If she's still there with you, this will be the case. If she was just too far gone to change, she will have long since left you, or you will have long since put her out. In that case don't you dare miss her. Why let's say it together. Ready?

"The bitch wasn't worth a damn. I glad she's gone!"

SAY IT AGAIN!

"The bitch wasn't worth a damn. I glad she's gone!"

Feels good doesn't it. It feels good because it was true. For the first time in your life you've come to grips with the truth about your ex-partner in misery. She's a cut out cancer. You were the surgeon. You cut away the damaged tissue. You'll survive now Mr. Black. You're on a roll. You're going to be a winner. You're almost ready for the big time. You're almost ready for a pleasant time. You're almost ready for a real woman, a civilized woman.

The more disciplined you are, the better able you'll wage the struggle. One of the things your woman is likely to do is try to defeat you by withholding sex. For a disciplined man, this tactic is a totally ineffective ploy. As a matter of fact, what you ought to do is immediately withhold sex from her. No sex until she's earned the right to have pleasure. At least no sex with HER. As long as this battle is on, as long as she is in basic training, no sex. Turn your back on her in bed. Spurn her overtures. Don't reward her outrageous conduct with sex. Let her know that her madness will get her a hard time, all the

time. I hope all the brothers are listening and listening good. Your battle efforts would be strengthened by joint operations, brother to brother. It undermines one man's attempt to get his house in order if another man is going to take your woman under his wing if she tries to escape your training. But imagine what would happen if no matter where she went, no matter who she turned to, no matter how high she pulled up that skirt, each and every Black man refused to deal with her. She'd have nowhere to run, nowhere to hide. It would become absolutely clear to her at that moment, her options are to get herself in gear or be lonely forever. In other words, she would know that it would be "dick on your terms or no dick at all"! To the extent that Black men do NOT see this as a joint military operation, and learn to cooperate with each other, your attempts to retrain are adversely affected. Don't misunderstand me, the training is rendered less effective but you may still be able to accomplish your objective. It'll just take longer to do it. Discipline is the key word here. If you aren't disciplined, you don't deserve victory. When "Ms. Sapphire" has run away from her man to escape his righteous "reconditioning", when in desperation she tries to sucker another Black man by "giving him the shot", that man is going to have to tell her to either
go to hell,
straighten up and go back to her man , or
eat shit and die.
All this will shock the living mess right out of her.

2

Now, you're either in her house or she's in yours. If you're in her house, start making plans to have another place on the side. By hook or crook, get another apartment or house! If the likely should occur, that is if she is not responsive to your emergency measures then tell her good bye and immediately read the Options chapter or drop me a post card. Help **IS** available. There are other women waiting for someone just like you.

If the place is yours, do the bitch at least the following favor. Keep her mother's phone number handy at all times. You may have to call her mom and let her know she's coming back to live there, perhaps with the kids. You're going to put her behind out the door right in the snow. She knew it was bad weather out there. If she didn't want to find herself in it, homeless, she should have kept her Black mouth shut and gone along with your new program. Shape up or ship out! This is it! This is the deal!

Gentlemen, one of the worse things you can do to yourself and your woman is permit them to remain in college. If a woman has more than two years college, she's probably ruined beyond repair. I had a friend of mine tell me years ago,

> *"there are no more scholars in college, just chumps looking for a job".*

How true this statement was. College has transformed itself from a pace where one inquires into the nature of man, the universe, God and truth, to factories into which you enter, repeat some nonsense you are told to repeat, take a test to make sure you've memorized the nonsense, get a piece of paper certifying you've past all the test, and then show that paper to a potential employer. The employer will have at best a person who is good at memorizing things and can follow instructions. He will not have a fully functioning *"reasoning machine"*. Our young people, men and women, enter college without first having a fully developed life plan of their own. In the absence of a plan, they take on the plan and philosophy of the school they're entering. Let me see if I can explain this further. When a man goes to Chiropractor school for example, he's going because he has a plan in mind. He wants to practice chiropractic medicine. All the while he's in the school, it serves to compliment and supplement his life's plan. That School of Chiropractic Medicine exist to serve him. He pays a fee of course but while he's there it's clear to him and to the school, why he's there and what the school should be telling him. Should he begin to receive formal instruction over a protracted period of time in nuclear physics, he'll know something is wrong. He'll withdraw because he clearly sees the school is inadequate for his purposes. It's not relative to his formalized plan. This clarity is at variance with what happens to Black young people who begin college undergraduate education.

67

Young people usually enter the campus with no idea of what they want to do in life. They have no well defined notions of anything at all, materially or spiritually. The result is that they take on the philosophy and direction of the school whatever that philosophy and direction may be. In other words, in the absence of their own plan, they're put on the school's plan. If the school is a white institution, a Black woman without a well formed plan will take on the plan of the whites. She'll receive her first indoctrination in how to divorce herself from the notion that her divine responsibility in life is to her husband and family. Such a view is definitely not part of the mainstream of thinking on today's campuses. If a Black woman is in an all Black college, she'll probably receive an identical indoctrination since most Black universities are spouting a white intellectual line. By the time a young woman is past her second year she will have become convinced that one of the more ignoble and disgusting avocations is that of a wife and homemaker. One friend of mine told me that he met a young lady about 23-24 years old who is a student at the Drexel University in Philadelphia (Philly, by the way, contains some uniquely screwed up women, although I hear D.C. women are worse). He described her as pretty, well built, well spoken and sexy. She told him that relationships were not on her mind, only her studies. Now at first this seems rather innocent and appropriate. If we analyze it a bit further we see that this young woman is already ruined. In her formative years, she has concluded that a man means nothing to her. That what is important is she enter the college, get the paper and work for the white man. Nowhere in this design sequence is there a place for training in her duty as a mother and wife. Her habits are being formed. College life today will prepare her for nothing other than being a laborer for whites. She will fail to include in her life's design, being a wife, mother, and good homemaker. Any man who pursues her as wife material would be making a mistake. What this girl is good for is laughs, conversation, going to the movies and sex. She will not be suitable as a wife. She may make an excellent whore but her sense of priorities and loyalties will not have been developed along the lines that foster commitment to a family unit. She'll probably go down in life as another one of those disgruntled, unhappy lonely career girls. You see, she went to college without a plan and so she got put on a plan. Are you mad at me women's libbers? Are you steaming hot right now? Do you think this writer is out of his ever loving mind? GOOD! He is. He's out of that former misery mind and into a peaceful productive mind. I could never have had the clarity of thought to write this book had I been with one of those cantankerous American Black girls. All my energies would have been spent dealing with her foolishness. But things are different now. My time is not being wasted.

3

Gentlemen, let's take a break. We've been at it for a while and we deserve a minute of rest. Let's give ourselves a hand. We're still hanging in there. We're holding on. We're primed. Why gentlemen, I just think that you're all excellent. You're good, real good. You're the true salt of the earth. You're the new and revitalized Black men of the hour. The Eskimo call themselves "Inuit" which roughly translated means "Man preeminent" or "The Man". Gentlemen, you're all Inuit. Shit on the white society because from now on out, by definition, YOU are "The Man". When you are finished reading this book and absorbing its principles, you will be well on your way to becoming the standard by which all other men will be measured. You've faced four hundred years of a hostile attempt to destroy you and you're still holding on. *YOU'RE STILL HERE AND READY TO KICK ASS!* Not only are you ready, you're actually doing it. Steady men. I've got more to come. Just hold on. I know you're ready to go take that hill, but hold on. You need a few more pieces of ammo before you move out. Hold on and keep the faith. Victory is yours for the taking. All you have to do is take it. It'll be hard work with lots of pain but if you take the pain, you'll deserve to take the prize.

CHAPTER-SIX

The
NEW-RECONSTRUCTION

"...awake, awake, utter a song: arise, Barak, and lead thy captivity captive..."

Gentlemen, we've talked about the negative nature of the American Black woman. We've talked about her unholy alliance with the white man. We've talked a bit about our complacency and passivity as Black men. I've hinted as to our contributory negligence as it relates to the state of mind of American Black women. We've talked about the activity of Black women and their assumption of Women's liberation doctrines. Let's begin the tedious process of putting this all together.

I propose to you the following proposition as a truth;

THE CURRENT DISAGREEABLE NATURE OF THE AMERICAN BLACK WOMAN IS THE FAULT OF THE AMERICAN BLACK MAN!

Yes gentlemen, the fact that the modern day American Black woman has a huge case of *"Bad Attitude-ites"* is the direct result of *OUR* failures as Black men. The ugly nature of the Black woman is a fact of life. It may be possible for a *few* of them to change. I don't think they will. I wouldn't bet my life on it, but I'll concede it may be possible for a very few of them to do it. Sometimes in life you make the type of mistake in which not only do you suffer, but another person suffers too. Generals go to the battle field and make mistakes. Their mistakes result in loss of life and limb. Yet the General knows that he has to move on. He has to learn by his mistakes. Tragic as his blunders may have been, he has to cut his loses and move on. He can't let the fact that he erred be a bar to further learning and progress. I think that in the case of our Black women, we as Black men

71

have been rather bad Generals. We've caused far too many casualties. *BUT*, we have to move on. We have to cut our losses, that is cut Black women from us and move forward. We can't afford to give up. We have to learn from our mistakes as we select a new group of women to share our lives. The General who screws up beyond belief is relieved of command. Black men in America have been *relieved of command* of the American Black woman, but we have not been relieved of command of other women in the world. It is *vital* that you understand this. The challenge we face is to take on another *"fire mission"*, so to speak, and not screw it up. By that I mean, take on the responsibility of other women who have no prior history with us, and therefore no reason to be hostile towards us. We'll discuss this proposed new mission in depth latter. So let's proceed.

Remember what that wise, elderly Black man I spoke about earlier said. He told me that in life, you are *"always under a plan"*. You're under your *own* plan, or someone else's plan. Gentlemen, as Black men, we failed to have a viable prosperity and protection plan for our women. The result is that in the absence of *our* plan, they jumped on board the white man's plan. The first thing I always hear from Black men when I tell them this is the old *"Barak, you have to understand, the white man has always been putting us down and making it hard for us."* routine. Of course I agree that whites have historically made it extremely difficult for us to be prosperous. But this truth is no excuse for not having at least, a *PLAN* for prosperity, even if you're going to be prohibited from implementing it. You ought to at least have the plan ready just in case you can use it. Gentlemen, when I see Black men out in the park from dusk to 3 and 4:00 *am*, under dim lights, playing basketball night after night after night, you're not going to convince me that these men are developing a contingency plan for prosperity. I'm not saying that these men typify the norm, but in general Black men don't have their mind on the task we have to face, the development of viable prosperity and protection plans for ourselves, our women and children and the implementation of same. The strange thing is, that I hear this *"you have to understand"* line from men who are skilled and accomplished businessmen. I can't understand why they are saying this. They've faced barriers to their personal progress but these barriers didn't stop *them*. They saw a challenge, mustered up the tenacity to deal with it, applied themselves, worked hard, and prevailed. They didn't give themselves any excuse. Racism didn't stop them. *Nothing* stopped them. Barriers don't have to stop anybody. There are many examples in the world today of minorities who are literally killed by the majority population but who still manage to be more prosperous than that majority. The Chinese in Malaysia are a good example of this. If I concede that we have faced problems, and I most certainly do, there is still no reason why we shouldn't have developed a contingency plan for prosperity to be put into effect at the most opportune moment. Don't be misguided by that last sentence however. The most opportune moment will never be under the most ideal conditions. The most opportune moment in history often occurs during a period of extreme distress. The creation of the small state of Israel is an example of this. Black people in America are about to be hit with some extremely distressful conditions. If you think it's bad now, it's going to get worse. But I argue that for us, this period in time is our most opportune moment. It's a time of motivation and you all know that it's hard to get Blacks to be motivated towards anything truly productive. The heat that will be turned on us just may motivate large numbers of Black men to take action like they've never taken it before. I'll concede that the *"you have to understand..."* argument is an acceptable one if it can be shown that we Black men have our minds on overall social, economic, spiritual, and military development rather than the three hundred slots available in major league basketball.[21] A Jew once said to me,

[21] The Philadelphia Daily News, March 4, 1992, quoted some statistics from The Center for the Study of Sport in Society as they relate to the odds against Black High School and College youngsters getting in to Pro Basketball and Football. The odds against both white and black high school youth getting into pro basketball are 10,345-1. The odds against Black high school children is 7,622-1. The odds against Black college players is 15-1. Only 38 Black high school players enter pro basketball each year. Only 38 Black college players enter the pro each year. The numbers are slightly higher for pro football.

"you know, in Russia, they [Russians] wouldn't hire us so we got around the problem by hiring ourselves."

Gentlemen, when the white man wouldn't hire us, we didn't hire ourselves. Oh Oh, that's one up for *'bad example being set for our women and children'*. We spent decades banging on the door of the white man begging for a job. We're still doing it. Now that's no plan for prosperity. It's a formulae for defeat. Oh Oh, that's another one up for *'bad example being set for our women and children'*. The *'begging for survival'* approach to a prosperity plan ask the very people sworn to destroy you, for their help in saving you. Oh Oh, that's yet **another** one up for *'bad example being set for our women and children'*. I don't see how anybody can respect us as long as we have these *'bad example'* strikes against us gentlemen, certainly not our women! You ought to be familiar with the writing of Marcus Garvey who founded the **Universal Negro Improvement Association** back in the early part of this century. Garvey was a Black man who understood the need for Black people to become totally independent of white society. He wrote,

> *"All peoples are struggling to blast a way through the industrial monopoly of races and nations, but the Negro as a whole has failed to grasp its true significance [of the struggle] and seems to delight in filling only that place created for him by the white man"* [22]

Garvey understood fundamental truths. He understood that we were engaged in a struggle, a war as it were. He understood that white American society was hell bent on the absolute control of the Black race and failing control, its destruction. He knew the absurdity of placing the welfare of Black people in the hands of whites for any appreciable length of time. He knew that in the final analysis, we as Black people would have to feed ourselves or not be fed at all. We would have to hire ourselves or not be hired at all. We would have to protect ourselves or not be protected at all. We would have to accept the responsibility we are supposed to accept, that is the

[22] The Philosophy and opinions of Marcus Garvey by Amy Jacques Garvey

responsibility for ourselves independent of white America. Garvey was correct. I'm only repeating the things he said in the 1920's. He was correct in the 1920's when he said these things, and I am correct now as I say them in 1992. I'm not ignoring the history of Black people in America. I'm not ignoring such phenomena as the KKK or the Jim Crow laws and all the other barriers to progress. I'm just suggesting that our focus and our energies have not been applied to true independence which precludes oppression. They've been applied to integration or restated, they've been applied to making appeals to our adversaries to elevate *us* at *their* expense. The logic of such an exercise escapes me. The fruit of such an exercise is nothing but more dependency on our enemy, rather than freedom from the enemy. If this has been our main thrust over the decades is it deserving of respect from our women? I think not.

Black people have skills in many areas. They are often the back bone of basic manual labor operations, assembly of parts, the service industry, the computer industry. Many black children are exposed to high-tech electronics just by fooling around with today's automobiles or video games. I've seen people fix their own VCR's, fix their own computer video games, use computers in their homes as a hobby, repair their own appliances, their own cars and much more. In every Black neighborhood, you have the jack of all trades types who can repair your porch, fix your roof, turn you gas and electric back on when it's been shut off, hook up free Cable TV for you. Years ago, I remember a guy who could provide you with free access to certain phone company options. These are all skilled people. All these skills can be an essential in an overall Black run industrial scheme. But back to the main point. Workers in a white corporation's computer room can't function if the computers are covered from top to bottom with piles of computer paper and tapes thrown on the floor and not cleaned up by the night maintenance crew who are usually Black. We're skilled enough for the whites to hire us as manual laborers. We should be skilled enough to hire ourselves for at least the same. We'll call up *Mr. White Plumber Incorporated.* He'll send out a Black man to do the job and charge us an outrageous fee. If that very same Black man came to us as an independent contractor, unaffiliated with the white company, we wouldn't give him the work. We'd have no confidence in him unless he worked for a white man. He'd have to be validated by the white man before he could be validated by us. Black women are very guilty of this. This is inexcusable. As Black men, we can no longer allow this to happen. When that hostile woman of yours turns down a Black independent contractor, it's up to you as a Black man to overrule her and hire him. It's up to this Black independent contractor however, to do the same quality of work for you that he'd do for the white man. He ought to do a better job for you than he'd do for the white man. I once knew of a couple young Black guys who 20 or so years ago worked in a paint factory. They were responsible for mixing up the chemicals used to make the paint. When their boss wasn't looking, they'd add hundreds of gallons of extra hydrochloric acid to the vats of paint as well as hundreds of gallons of other acids and harsh chemicals. They'd put this stuff in paint they knew was destined to be sold in white areas. In paint marketed for black areas, they'd make sure it was on the up and up. It's a rather drastic and perverse example, but it is nonetheless and example of Blacks doing a better job for their own than for the white man.

There are plenty of Black men and women with business acumen who would make fine industrialist. They can't get support from white Banks. They should be able to get it from the few Black banks around. They might be able to do so if Black people would support these Black banks. Blacks don't trust Black banks. There's an automatic assumption made in our minds that because the bank is Black owned and operated, it's certain to *"go under"*. It doesn't matter to us that the banking industry is collapsing, that Savings & Loan institutions have become a national disgrace, that there isn't enough money in the FDIC fund to back up banks should they fail. White banks are collapsing by the score but the we still put our faith in them. Put your confidence in a Black bank too.

If a Korean can sell you a toy trinket, *YOU* can sell the same trinket, made in the basement of some Black person's home. It'll be made by blacks, sold by blacks, and purchased by blacks. I know a young man who is about to embark on a major entrepreneurial effort in a West African Country. The thing has promise. It's so promising that people over there have been supportive of him. He'll probably put his project in full swing before the year is out. This guy will become rich and the people in the geographical area of his interest will have their standard of living greatly improved. The long term benefits of what he is doing will have a dramatic effect on the economy of that African nation providing he is able to completely shed any vestiges of corrupted Old World thinking. Yet he's a fellow who lives *"right on the block"*. He couldn't get his own kind here to support him. He finally had to go to Africa for support. Everything he's doing there could have been done here. The barrier was the reluctance of American Blacks to support another American Black. Gentlemen, this is a tragedy. This tragedy is **OUR TRAGEDY AND OUR FAULT.** This is also a tragedy of Black men failing to exercise command leadership over those Black women who are extremely reluctant to support any sophisticated Black, male run, enterprise. As Black men, we are supposed to be insightful, creative, far reaching, thoughtful, alert, vigilant, responsible, respectable, trustworthy commanders in charge at all times. We fall far too short on the scoreboard for all the above. I criticize myself for this also. You see, when we fail to establish viable economic structures for ourselves and our women, our women go for that structure, ever so imperfect, that they perceive to exist elsewhere. They've got to do something! If we're not doing it, they'll go where they think it *is* being done. Black men must insist first, that each and everyone of them buy from another Black person. Then insist that our women do the same. People from the Caribbean Islands come here to America, Koreans come here, everybody comes here with tremendous barriers and makes a good buck. There is *NOTHING* a Korean is doing that we couldn't have done. We're *RIGHT HERE* and do far less than what these racial groups are doing. We're still organizing to beg the white man for a crumb off his table. We lack true initiative and creativity. How can our women respect us if the sum total of our efforts is as mere organized beggars. How can our women look at us and think themselves proud to be associated with us if all we can do is band together and beg white trash to let us live side by side with them. What message do we send our women and children. It's clear to me what the message is. It's also clear to our women and children. We're telling them that we Black men don't think that we're worth anything. We're telling them that we think white trash is better than us. (One friend of mine told me Black people think "the white man's ice is colder"). We're telling our women and children that we can't stand on our own two feet. We're telling them that we need to *Integrate* because we don't think we can live without our *masters.* We have to have the white man around to think for us, and provide food and shelter for us.   I can remember the disgust I used to feel throughout the 1960's as I watched blacks on the news chanting *"2, 4, 6, 8, we wanna integrate".* It was enough to make me want to vomit. Gentlemen, it's no wonder that our women have become *"efficient".* By that I mean, they have cut out the "middle man", us! They've cut us out of the picture and done their bargaining with the white man directly. The fact is that they see themselves as getting a better deal from white society than the deal we got them. *GENTLE-MEN, OUR SHOES ARE MUDDY.* Gill Scott Heron said we're walking around like baby eagles in a chicken coup, that is, noble men acting like, and even believing ourselves to be buffoons.   The greatest problem we face is our own selves. We've got to shake off this *"dependency on the white man"* syndrome. That's Old World thinking. We have to get rid of it completely. I'll tell you this much, as a practical matter, you *WILL* get rid of it. You'll be forced to. White America is sick and tired of financing young Black girls and all the babies they're having.   White America is tired of giving up their jobs to Affirmative Action Negroes grinning ear to ear. They're going to clamp down and clamp down hard. Frankly, I take the position that this would be the best thing that could ever happen to the American Black. It would compel him to begin to depend on his own self or perish. Were there no Hitler, there would have been no Israel, at least not in this century. Hitler was the greatest motivator the Jews had. Danger motivates people. In Philadelphia, the candidacy of Frank Rizzo for Mayor brought Blacks to the voting booths in droves. Rizzo spelled danger in the minds of thousands of Black folks.

The ball is in our court as Black men. It's always been in our court. We've just let it sit there idle. The responsibility for the attitudes of our women and children rest on *our* shoulders. Our women are what we have made them. They are now paying the price for our ineptitude. I'll say it again.

The total responsibility for the development of a sound socio-political, economic, moral and defense frameworks from which Black people in America should operate is the responsibility of Black men.

The establishment of such frameworks has always been, is now, and will forever be, our duty and our duty exclusively as Black men. It's not the responsibility of white men, white women, or Black women to develop these frameworks. It's our job as Black men. We and we alone must organize and defend *the tribe*. We haven't done it. We're still begging the white man to feed and protect the tribe on our behalf. A friend of mine criticized me for advocating that Black men cast the American Black woman aside in favor of foreign women. He criticized my position on two grounds.

1. That it was a rejection of Black women.
2. That it failed to *"give Black women second chance"*.

I responded by suggesting that the issue of Black men rejecting Black women was a moot one. He should look at this issue in reverse. The fact is, that in significant measure, Black women have already rejected Black men. I'm merely suggesting that we stop trying to get them back and that instead we move on to more willing partners. As to the *"not giving them a second chance"* argument of his, it also falls flat when we consider the facts. Black men, as I have just said, failed in their responsibility to come up with a operational framework for life, under which Black women and children could prosper and be protected from harm. Women are reactionary. They're not creative. They merely respond to situations. Notwithstanding all the years Black women been with us, they're tired of waiting for us to develop and implement a viable prosperity and protection plan. They've seen Asians come here and prosper.

They've seen West Indians come here and prosper. They've seen everybody come here and pass right on by Black men. This progress of others is in marked contrast to Black men maintaining their unaccomplished status. It confuses the Black woman. The Koreans aren't about to take Black women in and Black women know it. The Jamaicans are clannish enough to have a system of male-female relations that is functioning and without need of Black American woman's input. So in the minds of Black women, the slave master, is her only hope. It's her best bet. After all there is a long standing tradition of the master dipping in the slave quarters for fun and frolic. Therefore in mind of the Black woman, the slave master is the most logical choice for a Black male substitute. Black women have looked at white society and decided that a prosperity plan existed on *that* side of the fence. They shifted sides. If there is to be any *"chances"* given, it's not Black men who are in the *"give a second chance"* position. It's the women who are in a position to give US a second chance. My argument is that they will not do it. I argue further that in the final analysis, it doesn't matter if they don't. What Black men must do is communicate with women who will give us the *"first chance"*. Another Black man told me that he thought if Black men "got it together", by that he meant developed a socio-economic structure that didn't depend on white society, Black women would then come back to us. He said it would take a lot of effort on our part to persuade them to return and we'd have to dangle a lot of glitter in front of their eyes. This would take a very long period of time he said. This may or may not be true but when a man get's in his 40's and older, he's not about to wait an inordinate amount of time for some Black woman to feel comfortable with him again. A 50 year old man doesn't want to waste his time. He wants to "make a move", and make it now. Most of the marriages that occur between American men and foreign women tend to be with older men. I think this will change as younger men, inspired by the principles inherent in The **New-Reconstruction**, settle down and accept the challenges of that movement. To the extent that American Black women desire to *"return to the fold"*, one might argue that this is a great thing. But again, what I'm saying is that we created a monster. This raunchy American Black women is the reactionary manifestation our failures as Black men. Even if she did want to return to the fold, assuming that our "fold" is now organized and prospering, I believe that all we'd have on our hands is a monster, temporarily tamed, but a monster just the same, and only temporarily tame. Our focus as Black men, can't be wasted on a futile attempt to reconcile ourselves with the American Black woman. We have to consider the long term issues at stake. We have to think of the next generation. When we bring in African, Asian, and Latin American women into our "tribe", of course we loose tribal affinity and relations with American Black women. You can effectively argue that by such an estrangement, there is a piece of every Black man lost. Yes, that's regrettable if we're considering our own narrow, selfish interest. But when we consider the broader question of our future, that is the future of the upcoming generations, we must be prepared to sacrifice the things that may satisfy us as individuals, in favor of what will satisfy future generations. These sacrifices we make, may have to include abandoning the notion of a reconciliation between ourselves and the American Black woman. I want to stress that the important thing is to take on non-hostile women as our wives. I've made it a point throughout our discussion to stipulate **American** Black women rather than just a Black woman. I want you to realize that the Black women in this country are not the only Black women in the world. I want to stress that we have choices for mates other than the American Black woman. We must invite into our lives women who have no reason to have ever been disappointed in us. Such women will make more functional mates. Once a woman has had reason not to trust you, she never will. Black women returning to the fold (those who might), will never really trust us again. At this point in history we need total, 100% absolute trust and unity in the home. Our primary *castles* must be secure and operational without fault. There must be no doubt about this. We'll need this quality of unity in order to meet the challenges of the new order, that is the **New-Reconstruction.** This quality of unity and support is a prerequisite for being able to deal with the, certain to come, onslaught of our enemies against our progress in the **New-**

Reconstruction. Do not enter the **New-Reconstruction** with even the slightest vestige of disunity or any other characteristic of the Old World Order. It'll ruin you, and undermine **New-Reconstruction** progress.

As Black men in America today, we can no longer afford to be *"half ass"* in how we think and how we structure our conduct. We can no longer afford to skirt and skim around fundamental truths. Our women don't respect us. That's a fact. We have not acted in ways that engender respect. This is a fact. You can talk and talk, and bull shit all day, but when the day ends, these facts, will still be facts. We have to be strong enough to accept these facts and act upon them. A political theorist once wrote,

> *"...We are opposed to a subjective approach to problems,....we must oppose ideas which are not based upon, or do not correspond to objective facts, because such ideas are fanciful and fallacious and will lead to failure if acted upon..."* [23]

The woman you choose as your mate must be 100%, unreservedly behind you. If she can not be 100% in your corner without reservation, you should not have her in your corner at all. The American Black woman will *never* be 100% behind you again in life. We've screwed up too bad. However, your **New World** wife will be behind you all the way, without question, because she will have no reason *NOT* to be behind you. You've no history of burning her or members of her 'tribe'. Just make sure you don't or you'll be right back where you started.

In the world of chemistry, there are a few standard ways used to describe chemical elements and compounds. These standard characterizations are recognized all over the world as "the right way to describe a chemical substance". One of the standard characteristics used to describe a compound or element is whether it can be dissolved in water or not, or the extent to which it can be dissolved in water. This characteristic is called the Solubility of the substance. For some odd reason, I used to get pissed off in college at having to say if this or that

[23] On Protracted War, Mao Tse-Tung

compound was soluble in water. I mean I used to ask myself "who gives a shit". I don't know why this used to tick me off but it did. I asked a professor of mine why it was do dammed important to determine if a thing was soluble in water. He said"

"Son, most of the Earth is water. Nature is efficient. Therefore most things that can be dissolved, can be dissolved in water since water is the most available substance. A Water Solubility index is a fine standard of reference we can use to describe the characteristics of a substance. You see son. it's all a matter of common sense."

Needles to say I felt like two pieces of bird crap. That professor was one of the coolest white boys I've ever known. He must have had some Black in him somewhere. His answer was beautiful. It was elegant and simplistic. It was fundamental. That one answer changed the manner in which I analyzed life. It made me appreciate what I now call the principle of '*the rock gut physics of life*'. There are some things that just make good, rock bottom, common sense." It's such rock gut, bottom line principles that serve as the underlying structure of the of the universe. The search for truth is a search for the fundamental rock gut principles which seem to govern the behavior of the universe. Now why am I going into all this! Well, Black women have acted in a rock gut, bottom line way. Black women accept as their standard for human behavior, the white man's morality and practices. From the Black woman's local perspective (by that I mean from the perspective her day to day life here in America), she seeks to be absorbed or dissolved into the majority "substance". The majority substance, as far as she is concerned, is White. White people are the numerical majority in this nation and therefore they constitute the majority substance to which she must be absorbed into, or dissolved by. The absence of any other mitigating conditions (like Black men having a viable prosperity plan of their own), encourages the Black woman to seek to be dissolved by the majority substance. Accordingly she goes the route of whiteness or the white material and moral structure. If you ask me, American white society has no valid claim to being a moral standard, but from the local perspective of the Black woman, it's appropriate to be dissolved by (absorbed into) them. How could this absorption have been prevented? Easy! Black men should have formed a minority substance whose forces of attraction would overcome the majority substance. For example, the Earth spins on it's axis at a fantastic rate but we don't go flying off in to outer space due to what you have come to know as the force of gravity holding us down. Gravity, is not gravity at all, in any 'hold me down' sense. It's the tendency of the center of mass of one object to be attracted to the center of mass of another object. The center of mass of our bodies is attracted to the center of mass of the Earth and keeps us pined down. Gravity counter balances the force that tries to throw us off into space. Sometimes I wonder if this counter balancing act has actually works. Pro-Feminist Black men talk like they've been thrown off the Earth and are on their way to the planet Pluto. What would have keep Black women tied to Black men, or to restate the question, what force applied to Black women, would have overcome their attraction to a white morality and prosperity plan? Why the answer is easy. A Black morality and prosperity plan! Blackness would have mitigated and overcome whiteness, had Blackness been 'on time'. In other words the song "We Shall Overcome" would not have been a bunch of bull.

No woman is a stand alone module. She always wants to be absorbed by something. You'll usually hear this expressed in terms like "I want a man to come along and take care of me" or "I just want to be held" or words to that effect. It all means that she wants to be absorbed by/into you. Can you imagine yourself as a Black man crying and telling some Black woman "Please hold me, I just want to be held." Of course not. Such a solicitation from the mouth of a man would be disgraceful. It runs against the natural order of things. It's a *woman's thing* (besides an American Black woman is likely to look at you, laugh, then move on). The Black woman sought to be dissolved by a "solvent", or that which will dissolve the "solute". She is the solute. The solute is that substance which is dissolved by the solvent. For example water is the solvent and sugar is the solute. As Black men, our solubility quotient was weaker than the white man in the eyes of the Black woman and as a matter of fact. We just weren't strong enough to dissolve the Black woman. Had the Black woman broke the boundaries of local thinking and considered the greater world at large, she would have realized that the majority substance is not white, but non-white. Most people in the world are not white. Had she done this, she would have included in her analysis of options, non-white morality structures as opposed to the perverted morality of whites. Her switch from us to the white man satisfies her immediate desire to be associated with prosperity. Even if whites permitted her to be absorbed/ dissolved, she would discover in short order that she had been dissolved by a nation of perverts. In other words, she would get screwed up anyway. Our job as men is to maintain a separation of ourselves from American whites and construct a framework for prosperity that is morally wholesome. The one must companion the other.

All races of peoples have faced obstacles of one kind or another. There have been some races who have overcome the obstacles which faced them, and some races that have not. The early American colonist overcame the obstacle of British rule. The Native Americans (Indians) did not overcome the obstacle of the imperialism and expansionism of early American settlers. Let's not go down in the history books like the Native Americans (Indians) have. We as a race have not faced what the Jews have faced. The Jews have caught more hell over the centuries then we are likely to catch. White people, here in America and in Europe, have *never* liked Jews. They've hated and despised the Jew way before they hated and despised Black people. Whites have engaged in systematic efforts not just to enslave the Jew but to eradicate him from the face of the Earth. Their efforts to this end have been both covert and by omission. In Hitler, the Europeans gave it their best shot. The Germans by direct action, sought to destroy the Jewish race. The rest of Europe, who knew what was happening in Germany, lent a helping hand to Hitler by not directly opposing his anti-semitic policies. When Jews were being beat and slaughtered in the streets of Pre-War Germany, who in Europe, who in the world stood up in outrage. Virtually no one. I'm not suggesting that anyone should have. In the final analysis, each race is *"on its own"*. It's every race out for itself. You've got to take care of your own tribe or it will not get taken care of at all. Smart Jews got out of Germany. Lucky Jews managed to get out after the Allied Occupation of Germany. Both groups founded Israel so that the bottom line became Hitler shot himself and they (the Jews) have the state of Israel. Dumb Jews, of course, died in the gas chambers. The world is full of paradoxes. Regardless of wether you like or dislike Jews, the fact remains that they are a sound example of resoluteness. They are a *"bad ass people"* who have learned to rely mainly on themselves and not depend on others for their security. No group wants to spill the precious blood of their tribe to save what they consider to be a bunch of no counts from another tribe. Accordingly the Europeans during the 1930's to 1950's were not willing to spill *their* blood for Jews. It's a similar situation here in America. White Americans are tired of expending their national resources on behalf of Blacks, who they imagine to be little more than entertainers and shiftless buffoons.

Both Black men and Black women contributed to the current hostile atmosphere which exist between them, but the ultimate responsibility for this condition falls on our shoulders as Black men. Remember our women are angry at us because of our failure to put in place a good Provide and Protect plan for them. We haven't tried hard enough. We've told ourselves that in the face of white resistance, Black independence is just too difficult a mission to accomplish. We've told ourselves that the only thing we can do is March on Washington and beg the white man for some crumbs off his table because we don't think we can bake a loaf of bread ourselves. We have to shape up. We have to grab the bull by the horns. We've screwed up but we can't labor that point. We have to cut our losses and move on, correcting our past mistakes as we go. I've talked to many Black men who though they no longer find it viable to think in terms of forming relationships with an American Black women, still can't seem to 'cut their losses' and move on. I can't put my finger on what is holding them back. One Black man told me that it was his feelings of guilt that held him back. He knew he couldn't work things out with the American Black woman but his sense of guilt over his contribution to her hostility prevented him from going forward. It's as though he wanted to be punished by keeping that hostile women around for a daily berating. Gentlemen, I'll say it again. We have to move on. We can't sit in the pool of our own urine and cry about how bad it smells. It may leave a big stain on the sidewalk, and we may not have the lysol and bleach to clean it up, but that's the unfortunate reality of our situation. We have to get up move on anyway. That young Black man I just mentioned is what I call a **"Stage-2"** man. I've seen Black men go through five stages of development as they relate to relationships with American Black women,

1) Conceding that the American Black woman is a horrible creature.

2) Thinking that he can change her nature for the better.

3) Realizing that he can't change her nature and resigning himself to a life without a mate.

4) Realizing his resignation in Stage-3 is unnecessary because there is an alternative to the American Black women in the form of women from other countries.

5) Actively engaged in the process of marriage to a non-American national.

You can't get a man to skip steps. Each of us will travel the road to and through these stages at our own pace and in our own time. I've spoken to hundreds of Black men between the ages of roughly 25 to 48 during the past few years. About eighty five percent of them are at **Stage-1**. Of the remaining 15 percent, one percent report that they have no problem with their Black woman. Of the remaining 14 percent they are about evenly dispersed between the subsequent stages. The important thing is for a man to move from stage to stage and not get stuck in any stage other than **Stage-5**. The black men I've talked to who have reached **Stage-1** and are on their way to the second stage, seem to get stuck for protracted periods of time at **Stage-2**. These are the men who are trying to make a rotte apple turn fresh again. Those stuck at stage one don't do themselves or anyone else any good by remaining there. You just can't be a chronic and constant complainer about Black women yet fail to take remedial action. Men at Stage-3 have become so frustrated that they've lost confidence altogether in their ability to remedy the situation. Men, You have to have the confidence that you can make things better. Marcus Garvey once said,

"If you have no confidence in self, you are twice defeated in the race of life..." [24]

As I said, Black men and women are now paying the price for the mistakes of Black men. Black men are paying the price of ineptitude in the form of having to contend with mad hostile Black women. The Black woman is, and will, in increasing numbers continue to pay the price of our ineptitude in the form of loneliness. We've been lackluster and so she's become hostile. She's become so irreversibly hostile that she's no good to anybody, not even herself. I foresee increasing numbers of Black women with no man.̇ They'll become the new disenfranchised class within America. **We Black men created a monster.** Now, we don't want her, and the white man *won't* want her either. She has become the victim of our *"not on the job"* training. Cruel as it may sound, we have to cut her loose even though her current mental state is *OUR* fault. We're not off the hook. We'll just might go down in history as screw ups. African men I know say *"you men don't take care of your women"*. They think we're screw ups who use white oppression as an excuse for inactivity, lack of creativity and weakness. The total ball of wax is in our laps. It was our responsibility to provide on an economic front, on a character front, and on a spiritual and educational front. I personally have a history of failure in all the above. I *KNOW* you do too. But it's not too late gentlemen, it's not too late.

I mentioned to you earlier that we have to change our ways. That young Black man I mentioned above who is setting up businesses in Africa told me he would spurn the overtures

---
[24]   The Philosophy and Opinions of Marcus Garvey, Amy Jacques Garvey

of any other American Black who would want to join him in his venture. I asked him why. He told me that Black men are screw ups and not responsible. He wasn't going to go thousands of miles across the sea for a fresh start and take with him men who have shown an unwillingness to act right. They'd only mess up over there like they messed up here. It was sad to hear this, but I couldn't fault him for taking that position. We are about to discuss options to the Black American woman but as I said before, if we don't change our ways, we'll wind up with millions of hostile African and Asian women at our feet. Feel guilty. Feel guilty because you screwed up and created the hostile Black woman. However don't let your guilt hold you back. Be strong, Admit your mistakes, apologize, be courageous. But above all, **move on!** Courage now requires that you take on the new woman, the foreign woman, women primarily of the so-called Third World who are untainted by a protracted American experience. Nature has already punished you for your mistakes in the form of the hostile American Black woman. Nature now is giving you a chance to start fresh with a woman who has no reason to be hostile to you. Your new women won't carry the emotional baggage one carries because of 400 years of slavery in America. She'll come here with an mind set unbiased against you. She'll come within the framework of a tender loving individual ready to share your life.

I've had many American Black women say to me,

> *"yeah, nature is giving you Black men a fresh start but how about us. We're stuck. No body wants us. What do we do."*

My advice to her was that nature was giving her a chance too. Nature would give her the chance to instruct her infant children in how to behave. Instruct your men in how to be responsible *"Commanders In Chief"*. Teach them how to be good providers for their families. Tell them that such is their primary duty. Tell them that there is no excuse for failure. Teach them to overcome obstacles rather than have obstacles overcome them. Condition them to see it as unacceptable to fail in your duty and then blame the white man or anybody else. Tell them the truth, that the white man is merely an obstacle. He's merely another obstacle to be overcome just as there will be other obstacles in life to overcome. Teach them to be warriors, to love a good fight, a good challenge. Teach them to be winners. Make them love the sweet taste of victory. They ought to have a fanatical obsession with obtaining the final victory over their enemies. Don't allow them to develop into another generation of Integrationist, that is to say, another generation of Black men whose only contribution to the goals of prosperity and protection takes the form of another march on Washington begging the white man for protection under his laws or begging for some crumbs off his table to eat. Teach him to bake his own bread and make his own table. Tell him that he and he alone has the obligation to defend himself, his women and his children. Tell him outright, that you will refuse to respect him, you'll disown him, should he fail to learn these lessons or turn into one of these misguided Integrationist beggars.

Instruct your girl children that men have large and fragile egos. Men have always been this way and are likely to be this way forever, but that in the final analysis, this characteristic of men is no real barrier to peace, harmony and prosperity within the family structure. Instruct them that part of their responsibility **IS** to accommodate a man's ego. Teach them to be a bit more thoughtful than they've been. Tell them that the ultimate joy in life is for a woman to apply herself to the task of mother and wife. Instill within her such a passion for family life that all else becomes an unsatisfying vocation. Admit to her the truth, that *you* are miserable because you don't have a man. You don't have that close knit family unit you want so very much deep down inside. Tell her of how inadequate your *career* has been as a replacement for a proper husband and father to your children. Take the time and talk to men of the **NEW-RECONSTRUCTION.** Put away your anger and dialog with them. Listen to what they say they want in a relationship. Listen to what they say they're getting from their new women. Because it's what they are now getting that you didn't give. It's the treatment they're now getting that makes them happy. This is what you failed to give them. Women, a happy man is a man that will treat you like a queen. They failed you and you failed them. Take the pain of these confessions and new inquiries. The future welfare of your children are at stake. Don't let them make the same mistakes that were m made in the past. The men are on a road to reconstruction and rebuilding. They've had to admit their failures. They are acutely aware that they can screw up again if they're not careful. They'll do well. They'll change. You won't be the beneficiary of their change, but your children can be. I'll admit that the disenfranchised Black women will not benefit herself from the **"NEW-RECONSTRUCTION"**, this period of reevaluation, revival, and rebuilding. Women, I'm going to be honest here. That's the only way I can try to help you. I can tell you that I've never treated any American Black woman as good as I treat my Asian wife. I've seen Black women who know me get burning mad as they watch how considerate I am of her, how affectionate I am with her, how valuable I consider her counsel to be. The treatment she gets is what Black women only dream about. My wife gets treated this way because she gives me the respect I think I'm due. I'm treated like the king of the castle in my house. Her loyalty to me has been put to test several times and she's come through with shinning honors. She deserves good treatment from me. She's all the things to me that you never were. As I said earlier, if you can be objective for once in your life, if you can put your anger aside for one hour and look at why men in my new circumstance are happy with their wives, you'll discover the secret of what your contribution to a relationship should be. Black women, **PROVE ME WRONG!** Show me, show the world, that you can make a change. You can be humble and dutiful. You can place family above the diversions this society has placed before you. I say you can't do it. But that's just my personal opinion. Prove me wrong. I want to be wrong. However, I can't say I'm wrong if I'm not and so far I'm not. You're all evil. You're getting worse. Shahrazad Ali asked you to change and you didn't do it. I don't think you can and until I see evidence that you are, I'll continue to say that you're beyond redemption.

Black men failed to create institutions which served

the interest of their own kind. Black women jumped off the boat of ineptitude and went to where they thought prosperity was. They're finding out, or will find out that the prosperity on the other boat is not for them. They only hold a piece of it "pro temp" until they serve the purpose of the white man. Let's keep our minds on reconstruction, on rebuilding, on correcting our mistakes.

Men, we've talked. Now we have to act. We're happy in the knowledge that we're not alone in our thoughts about the American
Black woman. We're glad to see that

"there's someone out there like me who understands
what I'm going through with that Black woman of mine"

We're not too happy with the fact that we're being told we've acted like passive chumps, buffoons, irresponsible weaklings, and all around jerks. We're not happy with the fact that it's being said the whole problem we're having with American black women is *our* fault. We still want to squirm and try to put the blame solely on women's shoulders and the white man. We don't want to accept the fact that our women have merely reacted to the phenomena of our ineptitude. Put this book down for a minute and reflect. Truth hurts. I told you at the outset it was going to hurt. I wrote this chapter and wept. It was just all too true. I couldn't take it, but I *HAD* to take it. I had to be what I wanted you to be, that is, courageous and accepting of truth. I've been lucky. Nature gave me my second chance. My wife is Asian. I have a fresh start. I've got to change my old ways. I leave behind me a legacy of women to whom I've caused misery. I can't go back and change that, but I can do the right thing with what I now have. Gentlemen, this is not time for bullshit. I've got to tell you this. I've got to admit this about myself because I don't want to hear any bullshit from you either. I don't want to hear you talk mess and try to make excuses. If I hear it, I'm going to get mad and out of love for you, I'm going to kick your ass, or you're going to kick mine. I don't want you to accept bullshit and excuses out of me, and I don't want to accept it from you. I want us all to join in and take the pain. I want us all to be a support system for each other. I want us all to identify and make known our talents. I want Black men to hire Black plumbers, Black electricians, Black lawyers, Black grounds keepers etc. I want you to seek each other out and discover what you all can do for each other. Support each other. I want you to get out of that *"don't hire a nigger, he can't do the job as good as a white man"* mentality. I want you to get out of that *"aww, it's only a nigger, I won't do as good a job for him as I would for the white man"* mentality. I want our next group of women to walk out of their doors and go to a Black owned store and a Black run school and a Black run factory. *All created by Black men. I want our women to be able to say "whites? They can't do for me more than what my Black man can".* I don't want this next group of women coming in forced to be hostile to us too. In short, I want White man spelled with a small "W". I'll keep spelling Black with a capital "B".

This whole issue of relationships is more important than you realize. The consequences of a successful or failed Black male female relationships are confined not only to the particular couples involved but also to the life and death struggle of *"Our Nation"*. When I say Our Nation, I'm talking about Black people in America. Our nation's territory consist of all those areas where we occupy the land. We don't yet own it, but we can in time with proper planning. I had one Black pervert say to me,

"man you're crazy to think we can ever seize and own territory here in America. The white man wouldn't let us"!

That young Black man was a prime example of someone raised on a strong diet of TV. The fact is that we DO hold vast areas of land right now. These areas are commonly referred to as Inner City areas or to put it more explicitly, Ghettos. We've held these territories but we haven't put our minds towards its proper maintenance. We've been distracted by the diversionary tactic of the white man. Gentlemen, if we had our women in check, our children under control, our own means of manufacturing and production, we'd be divorced from the white man. As it stands now, we're still his suckers and entertainers.

We've been at war with our women, because we're at war with the whites who have made our women their allies. Our passivity permitted this to happen. As Black men, we can still win the war. We can reverse the current status quo which can best be characterized as whites manipulating for advantage and Blacks passively reacting, to their own disadvantage. The unholy alliance I spoke of earlier between our women and white society is a grand diversionary tactic. Black men's minds are diverted from real progress by this secondary conflict with their women. The primary conflict is your war with white America. We must not fall for the diversionary tactic. The fact that this tactic is so successful is due to our failures as Black men to counteract it. It has been, and still is, the overall mission of white society vis a vis African Americans to repress us. As I said earlier, the ball is really in our court. All we have to do is get off our asses and pick it up. We don't have to fall victim to every diversionary tactic out there. Parents don't have to give in to their children's pressure for new toys and expensive sneaks every week. You see, even our children are completely caught up in the diversion. They're raised up with a strong diet of TV advertising. It's a diet most certain to keep a child's mind from developing along the lines of an independent thinker and precludes him from being able to objectively analyze the condition he is in. Where have the Black men been when these TV bullets have been flying? Where have we been and what have we been doing while our children have been under such an assault. We've been at the basketball court, at the gym, at the local watering hole etc. The enemy has been activity recruiting our women against us. The enemy has been actively assaulting and perverting the minds of our children. What have we been doing all this time? Effectively *Nothing!*

Gentlemen, our mission should be clear. It is to survive and prosper. Everything we've been doing so far has worked against our mission. We've been working against our own interest. The murder rate in our communities is astonishing. So a question can be raised as to whether we are surviving.

All across America, Black people are poor and getting poorer by the day. We certainly are not prospering and you won't prosper as long as you think the way is through entertainment. That's not the way the majority of **The Nation** will be able to accomplish our mission. Heaven forbid that we should ever achieve prosperity by becoming the entertainer class for the world, singers, dancers, hoop throwers and gladiators. Do you want us to become just one giant entertainment troupe for the world?

As I mentioned to you earlier, we are at a critical time period in our history. Our very survival as Black men is at stake. I can't stress this enough. A friend of mine and I were discussing the issue of Black male-female relationships this very day. He conceded that shortly Black men would divide themselves into those who would begin to look elsewhere for women and those who would give these Black American women a *"second chance"* as he put it. I told him that our primary obligation, given the particulars of our circumstances, is to ourselves as Black men first. At this point in history, the notion of Black men giving Black women a second chance is moot. We don't have time for that and as a practical matter, *we* were the screw-ups. We aren't in a position to give *anybody* a second chance. It's nature who is giving **US** a second chance by allowing us to partake of the **New-Reconstruction** and it's great goals.

We Black men are the Officer class of our race here in America. In the face of the tragedy we have experienced here, we officers have to keep ourselves in tack and re-group. The survival of The Nation depends on it.' As an example of this principle I'll use the policy of the German High Military Command towards the end of WWII. They knew the country was about to fall. They knew chaos would follow. The Nazis had screwed up royal. The German High Command were fashioned after the mold of old Imperial German Army Officer Corps under the Kaisers (German Emperors). They drew a class distinction between themselves and the Nazis who they considered to be nothing more than brigands and criminals (they were correct). It became their position that at that moment in history, more important than anything else, was that the

German Army survive intact, in particular the Officer Class. I say we Black men are in a similar position now. White America and their Black women allies, are moving against us. This very morning word has come down that a Black woman, in alliance with the whites, has convicted Mike Tyson of rape. We can't waste time. It must be our immediate concern that throughout this onslaught by the whites and their allies, we as Black men *remain intact* as a social class, a class of officers as it were. We need to be around to regroup and conduct the **New-RECON-STRUCTION.** We'll have to cut that Black women from us and consider her a battle casualty. Tag her and bag her in your mind. See her as shipped off to the morgue. Don't waste anymore of your time with her. *WE* must remain intact as a viable force. *WE* Black officers are the future. **Gentlemen, Close Ranks!** I can't stress enough, how important it is for Black men to coalesce. They're picking us off one by one. Tyson is just the most recent and public example of this. The former Mayor of Washington D.C., Marian Barry was yet another. One by one, they're trying to bring down our Black officers (unfortunately our officers are making themselves easy targets, but this is a subject for another book) Men must form unions of men whose purpose is a solid defense of Black men against the current onslaught. Let no one attack us and go unpunished.

The recent decision in the Rodney King police brutality case should by now make the arguments I give in favor of a separate parallel Black socio-economic-defense system more palatable. The entire world saw and condemned the excessive force used against Rodney King. The naked racism of America had been exposed to the entire of the world. The London press said they could not distinguish America from South Africa. The French press appropriately condemned Americans for citing other nations for human rights violations while clearly being guilty of the same. The white jury in the case freed the four police officers on trial for the brutality against King. Newspapers around the world expressed shock at the verdict. The outrage on the part of the Black community was unmeasurable. Following the jury exoneration of the police offices, Black residents took to the streets with that now famous chant *"No justice, No peace"*. They took their vengeance out on the symbolic representatives of those who had disrespected and oppressed them. One police officer conceded that the jury decision was *"a clear signal that we cops can do whatever we want to Back males and get away with it"*. Rioting spread to several cities across America and protestors took to the streets in several foreign countries. Young Black men beat, killed and destroyed without mercy. The destruction reached the star studied streets of Hollywood. I make no apology for the conduct of the people. Where the burden of injustice has become too much to bear, where the peaceful protestation of people are ignored, the nation can expect nothing other than what happened. I am convinced that if for each act of violence perpetrated against us as a race, for each act of judicial or political injustice against us by white Americans, there would follow an immediate and violet counter reaction, you would find fewer and fewer cases of barbarism on the part of Americans perpetrated against us. For every black man beat without mercy by white cops, ten white cops should be made to know the *"peoples justice"*, or restated, the justice of **The New Reconstruction.** Officials guilty of such crimes should be arrested by officers of the **New Reconstruction**, tried by **New Reconstruction** Courts, and punished according to New Reconstruction laws. Of course, we would be more than willing to return the bodies of these perpetrators back to white America for burial.

Let this nation see we are **not** divided, but united in our determination *NOT* to go out like chumps but to prevail. These unions of men will serve also as a platform for Black men to discuss issues specific to their present condition. They will put forth the Black men's agenda. Such unions are a needed support system. It'll be like a huge fraternity, a grand brotherhood. Kappa didn't really do anything for you. Neither did Omega, But a national, unified Brotherhood of Black men can. Let no man enter the brotherhood who is pro feminist. Let no man enter who is not willing to shed the vestiges of his past weakness, and take on a new nature, a strong resolute nature. Let these men enter under a sacred oath of loyalty to the cause they define as appropriate for themselves. Let the cause include the exaltation of Black men and the rebuilding of **The**

Nation. Let men who are strong instruct their weaker brothers who are eager for a change. Let the cause include the building of strong and impenetrable basic family structures. I condemn weak Black men who once their weakness is made known to them, continue to be weak. I support the weak who were weak but sincere in their desire to make a change. I look up to those men who are stronger than I and ask of them their guidance. I am willing to learn, willing to develop.

If Black men fail to survive the American experience, there will be absolutely no one left to reshape our communities. We will continue to degenerate into further states of barbarism and finally extinction. We must survive as a class, re-group and rule. Destiny calls upon us for this purpose. God calls upon us for this purpose. The angels in heaven call upon us and urge us forward. Throughout the heavens there is great and thunderous applause in our favor. We must regroup. We must mount a counter offensive. We must prevail. We must gain the victory and rule over our houses. This is *our* Manifest Destiny. Let the Sons of Heaven be exalted in the eyes of the universe and let our enemies kneel at our footstools. We are the true Sons of Heaven. The eyes of creation are watching us to see what we do. Gentlemen, we have to perform. We have to unify. Recently, one young Black man conspired with a Black woman against me. He doesn't know that I know. Such a man is a disgrace. Let no man of the brotherhood be guilty of such thing. Let such a man be ostracized from the community of Black men. Let ostracizing be a horror of horrors, something too terrible to bear. Let it be so terrible that the poor dumb bastard will want to commit suicide. Let him be marked as a traitor, an enemy, a conspirator with the white man or the white man's agent. Such a Black man is an enemy far more dangerous than the whites because he is in our midst. Such a disgraceful Black man must get his proper due, that which has always been reserved for traitors.

Gentlemen, this may all sound scary but as I said before we're in a scary time period. We're in a crises. It's time for us to act like men and clean house. We must start with ourselves. Each of us is our very first *"own House"*. We start by cleaning up ourselves and letting our own kind know that we mean business. This is no time for bullshit. Gentlemen, this is a call to arms. I sound the trumpet. Who will answer the call? Must I go into battle alone? Must I hang my head in shame before my enemies when they call you cowards. Should only a few of us feel strong enough to take on the responsibility of the **New Woman**? It's a call to arms gentlemen. Take up the challenge. Don't go out like a bunch of faggots.

The white man is excluding us from whatever participation in American society we were engaged in. A cap is being put on the number of *"Negroes of Note"* as a friend of mine says. A cap is put on the number of non white people who will be permitted to play on the white stage of American life. This cap has a sealing of zero participants, in other words, the new rule is *No Blacks Allowed.* All that can be done to keep Blacks from prospering in America is now being done. Black women are partners with the white man in this effort. As I said before, it is going to be important that we of the Brotherhood, that is we Black officers, think totally anew. We've got to think in terms of a parallel reality, parallel socio-economic and defense structures independent of white society. I talked to a friend who had little confidence that this could be achieved. I had to explain to him that we had all the necessary ingredients lined up. We have Blacks who are in fact consumers in an existing white consumer market. We have Blacks who have worked for whites in capacities ranging from corporate executives to street sweepers and everything in between. We've got me money to buy things. We just pump our money back to whites and parcel a fair amount out to the Koreans (we've got our wallets and pocket books wide open for any member of the United Nations to put their hand in and scoop out the coins, any member except an African member that is. We don't want to give anything to another Black). We have the technical expertise to build things. This friend suggested that after Blacks were excluded form American society, they would still be solicited as consumers for white products. In other words we wouldn't be permitted to advantage ourselves of the overall society but we would be permitted to support it. I say nonsense on this. Men of the Brotherhood, fellow officers, gather together! *Think! Talk! Create! Build! Work hard!* We don't need white America to survive. When we take on the New Woman, the women of the New-Reconstruction, let's also be creating a system of living and values designed by us, for us, and in our best interest. I know I've spoken of this earlier but it can't hurt to go over it again.

I make the following long term predictions:

1) The white women's movement will be stopped dead in its tracks within the next 10 years. White males are right now, just letting these women ride the crest and have all the fun they can. But in the final analysis white men are not going to let their women run over them. When the women's movement gets too far out of hand, white men will reel it back in even if it means kicking ass. The Thomas hearings were a manifestation of this. The white man really didn't care about Thomas. They weren't defending *HIM*. That entire thing was about white men showing women that they weren't going to be permitted to have Women's Lib issues and agendas preeminent over those of men's concerns. They were not going to permit a woman and her feminist supporters bring down a man. If it meant supporting Mr. Black nominee, they would have to support him to get that point across. Women who were astute recognized this. In other words what white men said to women was,

"Shit on you. We don't mind giving you a little bit of something but I'll be dammed if you're going to run our whole show. Just so you get the point, we're gong to let Judge Thomas on the court in spite of the fact that we believe he's guilty as hell. But if his crime was sexual harassment of that bitch, we don't care. She's only a bitch".

That's the real message of the hearing's outcome gentlemen. Those white men on the panel knew that they were in a state of war. They showed women that unless they are prepared for some hard core battle, they will be halted. The white men are almost reaching their point of saturation. Women's Lib is soon to be over. The white man will restore order to his house. But even when the Libbers are stopped they'll still be better off, by their reckoning, than how they were a few decades ago. White men will be happy. They will have stopped the woman's movement. White women will be happy. They drove this thing as far as they could and got as much as they could and they'll be happy with what they've gotten out of it these past few decades.

    2) Black woman will continue to ride the coat tales of white women's libbers. Black women think, erroneously, that the forward momentum of the women's movement has no limit, has no end. They don't realize that when a stop is put to white women's "progress" under the Women's Lib movement, a stop will be put to them too within the white world. The dust will settle and white women will turn on Black women with a viciousness they never dreamed of. The white women will cast them aside. Black women employed will be subject to massive dismissals in favor of white women. Black women will see that their "white sisters" were only using them as front line troops in sporadic battles to establish gains for white women. It was a white woman who came to Anita Hill and persuaded her to begin that fight against Judge Thomas. That white woman had an agenda. It had little to do with Hill. Hill was just an instrument to be used. When the anvil is lowered on Black women, it will be lowered twice, by whites and by Black men. We will have long since replaced her with African, Asian, Latin American or Caribbean women as part of the **New-Reconstruction.**

    3) Black men all across America, without distinction as to social rank, education, profession, or the lack thereof, will have divided themselves into two fundamental groups, The first group represents the old way, the way of the past. This group will consist of pro feminist Black men, unrepentant faggots, mental weaklings, scum who by word and deed show that they still revere the white man or at the very least can't shed their white induced social and psychological conditioning. These are the Black men who will continue to be duped by whites. This group is fit only for servitude and a hard time. I am confident that in the not too distant future they will experience either. If I had my way, I would place these kind of Black men in actual slavery and work them to their deaths. Such is the fate a misguided, weak, traitor deserves. Make no mistake gentlemen, you've just as much a dangerous enemy in the form of misguided pro feminist, pro-fag, weak, Black men as you do in the form of their white counterparts. The former is more dangerous because he lives right next door to you and can tell his masters all about you. These traitorous scum will get the inevitable justice which awaits them. The study of history clearly demonstrates this. When one of these scum reveals himself to you, don't you trust him. He'll sell you down the river as quick, if not quicker than a Black woman. Mark that man in your mind. Mark him well! Keep him on your shit list for latter processing. Gentlemen, let lines of distinction be drawn. You're of the **New-Reconstruction**. He's still *"a slave in Babylon"*.

The second, more progressive and enlightened group are those of the **New-Reconstruction**. These are the men of the Brotherhood. These are the men who are working on themselves. They are re-evaluating their old habits and objectively determining their value or lack thereof. They're altering their ways and redefining their status and position in America. They are inviting women to joint them who are untainted by the American Experience. They are the new family men who provide and protect their own. These men are so informed, so enlightened, that those of them who may be police officers for example, will refuse to work along side of other officers in the habit of disrespecting Black people. This type of police officer will prohibit and demand redress from any white officer who wantonly kills another Black person unjustly or otherwise abuses our women and children. The men of the brotherhood will be found in many levels of the working world. They will always go that extra mile to accommodate another member of the Brotherhood. They see themselves as in the white man's jobs for a short time period only. While they are there, they will do all they can do to subtly rip the white man off in favor of their own kind. They know they're last hired and first fired so they'll grab *all* they çan, *while* they can. Simultaneous with this, the Brotherhood will support efforts of other Black spiritual, military and businesses leaders. The goal is that at some time in the future, Blacks will work with, and for Blacks. The only Blacks to be found in white structures will be the scum dog, Black lackeys of the white man or the spies of the Brotherhood. As I mentioned to you earlier gentlemen, you have to get ready for battle. There's no gain without pain. We must be prepared for all stages of our **New-Reconstruction** including the attempts of our enemies to discredit, undermine and destroy our efforts. One famous writer and military strategist wrote that you ought to be prepared for struggle in three stages;

1. **The period of the enemies strategic offensive and your strategic defensive,**
2. **The period of the enemies strategic consolidation and our preparation for the counter-offensive,**
3. **The period of our strategic counter-offensive and the enemies strategic retreat. 25**

Gentlemen, I propose to you that in an overall historical context, Black people in America have lived through stage one. We are about to embark upon stage two. However, we must be prepared for what will appear to be another stage one. Our enemy will suddenly launch an all out attack on us in an attempt to thwart the **New-Reconstruction** before it gets off the ground. As far as these whites are concerned, the worst thing that could happen is Black men and their mates getting along and being productive. The enemy will do anything to prevent this from happening. The more disruptive he can be to Black family unity the better it is for him. The eyes of the world will be watching us. The women of Africa, Asia, Latin America and the Caribbean who we invite to join us in the **New-Reconstruction** will be watching us. We will prove ourselves to be worthy of the mission we care called upon to undertake, worthy of prosperity, worthy of this holy hour, or we will show ourselves to be cowards deserving of contempt and disrespect from the entire of creation. I'm sure you remember the Prime Minister of Japan remarking in 1991 that the problems of America would be solved if it got rid of its Black people. He thought we were shiftless and lazy and unproductive. This is

25 Selected Military Writings of Mao Tse-Tung, On Protracted War.

the image much of the world has of us. It's predicated upon both the propaganda of the Americans as well as foreigners who get first hand impressions of us when they visit America. But gentlemen, we're on the road to a reconstruction, a renaissance of our spirit and our ways. Such a renaissance will lead to a revitalizing of our material conditions. **THE NEW-RECONSTRUCTION IS ON** gentlemen. Give a hand for God, Nation, decent women, and righteous, functioning, loving families.

CHAPTER-SEVEN

You Have Options

1

Men, I'm ready to discuss alternatives. I hope I did a good job of discussing *"responsibility **before** alternatives"*. In a future book, I'm going to be discussing options for the disenfranchised American Black woman as I call her. I'm going to show her that it doesn't have to be as bad for her as she may think. She **can** have a man. But such advice as I may have for her on this particular subject lies outside the scope of this book and is reserved for another publication.

We're going to discuss meeting women from other countries. This is not the obscure impossible task you may think it is. Thousands of American men each year take the road of marriage to non-American nationals[26] (see footnote and or .Appendix D for more information). The director of an agency

[26] For detailed information on immigration to America under the various visa classifications consult; Statistical Yearbook of the Immigration and Naturalization Service, U.S. Immigration and Naturalization Service, (U.S. Government Printing Office, Wash. D.C. This document contains hundreds of charts and tables and is a wealth of statistical data on immigrants to the United States. I took a look at the years 1984 to 1991 with a particular interest in foreign immigration for the purpose of marriage (K-1 Visa, Fiance' of American citizen). The total number of immigrees for that purpose for example of Philippine nationals has increased by 9.2 percent since 1984. The number of persons immigrating under the K-1 visa, all countries considered, has steadily increased by 12 percent from 1984 to 1990. See Appendix D for more information. American men are in increasing numbers choosing the option of foreign women as wives. A professor at the University of Texas, Sociology Dept., Dr. Davore Jadlicka, has studied the difference between American men who have married Asian Non-American nationals and those who have married European Non-American nationals. His study includes an analysis of public reaction (The Family Society and the Individual, 7th Edition). Contact, Dr. Davore Jadlicka, University of Texas, Sociology Dept, 3900 University Blvd., Tyler Texas 75799. Consult notes in this book and elsewhere for Dr. Jeanne Lin's study on conflict resolution in marriages between American men , all races, and non-American women.

called <u>Asian American Worldwide Services</u> that assists American men all throughout the process of selecting an Asian bride and partner for life, advised me that roughly one third of her male clients were African American men. I'll mention this agency again giving you some particulars.

If you know some women from other countries already here in America, ask them to give you the names of friends or relatives they think may be interested in corresponding with you. If you don't know any such women, join one of the many Pen-Pal clubs whose job it is to introduce you to ladies from around the world. These agencies have many services the least of which is providing you with photo's, names and addresses, and brief biographical sketches on ladies interested in forming relationships with American men. One agency I'm thinking of, charges a small ten to twenty dollar fee for sending you ten to twenty such "bio Stats" and photos. The agencies usually advertise in many magazines such as Popular Electronics, New York, Popular Mechanics, some computer Magazines and a host of other publications. I'll list a few in my footnotes. This is your beginning, getting some names to write via a lady already here or a pen-pal agency. Decide the type of woman to whom you want to be introduced. You may have a preference for African or Asian or Latin American or whatever. You may want to touch base with women from all these areas. You'll be intrigued with their similarities and their points of difference.

Let's discuss a few.

ASIAN LADIES

Individuals within a given culture manifest variations of the cultural norm. Likewise within the continent of Asia, you will find variations, country to country, of what we in the West think of as a typical Asian cultural norm. There is however, a fundamental set of characteristics that *are* universally Asian. Asian women irrespective of their particular country within the Asian continent share these common characteristics. We're going to briefly discuss the Asian ladies. The odds are that if your interest is in an Asian lady, you're going to be dealing with someone from the Philippines, Thailand, or Malaysia. More than likely you will be dealing with a Philippine lady. Accordingly, it's the women of this country I'll be using as the basis of my discussion.

The Philippine government has been alarmed at the rate their women have been making an exodus from the country and marrying men from other countries. In 1991, Cori Aquino (President of the Philippines) banned agencies who were engaged in introducing Philippine women to 'foreign' men. Such agencies also helped facilitate the paperwork necessary for Philippine national's marriage to foreign men. The publicly stated reason for the ban was the reported mistreatment these women were receiving once they immigrated to other countries. This alleged mis-treatment is not supported by any research I've conducted, nor have I heard of any significant mis treatment cases from agencies or Philippine women.[27] I suspect the real reason was had more to do with an issue of national pride. The Philippine government was concerned about an injury to their prestige. A massive exodus of women might be seen as an indication of the government's inability to provide a satisfactory standard of living for their citizens. I believe the rate of exodus, if unchecked would have eventually drained the resources of the nation. I mention this only to encourage those of you about to consider marriage to a Philippine national, not to be historically Black about this, that is, not to procrastinate. There may come a time when the Philippine government forbids citizens to exit the country.

My first caution to you is to be very careful about taking an interest in ladies who work on or near a military base. You veterans out there will understand exactly why I say this. You don't want to get involved with a girl who has been a *"number one good time"* girl for the GI's. You might as well pick up and marry an Atlantic City hooker or better yet, keep your American Black woman. Neither of them make good life time partners as is required in a marriage. Keep in mind at all times that your objective is to select a woman for the purpose of marriage. The qualities you should be looking for must be those

[27]   See Marital Satisfaction and Conflict in Intercultural Marriages, Dr. Jeanne Lin, 1990, study conducted through the Univ. of Washington, Seattle Wash.

commensurate with being a good wife and mother. I spoke to one young Black recently who began to extol the virtues of he girl he just met. He was thinking of her in terms of marriage. He began to tell me of her *'potential'*. The first problem occurs with the word *'potential'*. Gentlemen, you don't marry *'potential'*. Potential is *'tomorrow'*. You marry what you see in front of your face *today!* You may not know what tomorrow brings but you can sure see what's happening to you today! The woman you marry because of her *'potential'*, in all likelihood will *NOT* develop along the lines you want her to. She is what she is at the moment you meet her. Evaluate her on the basis of what you can see, not what you *think* she might be in the future.

The young man continued by telling me how intelligent this Black girl was, and of her acceptance into a Doctoral program at a leading university. He was impressed with the fact that she worked out at the nearby Health Spa. She also did a lot of reading he said. He went on to describe a few more of her *'virtues'*. When he finished running his mouth, I asked him the following questions about the girl;
1. can she cook,
2. can she keep a clean house,
3. did she have a well developed maternal instinct, that is, does she like children and would she be a good mother.

Astonishingly he didn't know the answer to any of these questions. I suggested to him that all the things he told me about her meant absolutely nothing. I also suggested that the only thing which mattered when it comes to evaluating a woman as a potential life time mate is whether she has the qualities requisite for that job, the job of a wife homemaker and mother of your children. All else is bull! The fact that she may be Ms.Ph.D personified, or that she can barbell you to death at the Health Spa means *absolutely nothing!* The fact that she may have read five million books last summer means absolutely nothing! The only important questions are, can she cook, keep house, bear children, raise children, be considerate and compassionate, and follow the directives of a man. These things, and these things alone, are all that matter. I hear from plenty of men with intellectual wives, Health Spa wives, this, that and the other kind of wives, but each of these husbands is miserable. Their wives can do everything *except* the things that really matter to a man, and to a family unit. So keep this in mind as you evaluate women. Don't get side tracked by her peripheral characteristics. At one point my policy became not to date any girl who had more than two years of college. Two years was enough to corrupt her and turn her into a high testosterone feminist. I have one friend of mine who taught at an Ivy League university tell me his policy was not to date girls with more than a High School diploma. His contention was that anything more than high school was enough to corrupt a woman's soul. Keep your focus on a woman's primary characteristics. Does she have a well cultivated *"common sense"*. Can she cook, clean, raise children and follow instructions.

As you evaluate Asian ladies, you're going to become aware of slight differences in temperament and attitude between those who live in major cities like Manilla and those who live in the more rural areas. My personal preference is for ladies from rural areas. My thinking goes something like this;

1. **American society is corrupt.**
2. **White Americans are degenerate.**
3. **The Americans in the Philippines live mainly in or near the cities.**
4. **A lady with too much unsupervised contact with these degenerate Americans may have picked up some of their degenerate ways.**

Of course these points are only something to *think* about as you begin your evaluation of the ladies. It is by no means etched in stone that the ladies of the cities are *certain* to be as affected as I suggested. But don't dismiss this as a possibility as you scrutinize the ladies you will meet or otherwise correspond with.

You will discover that the Asian women are remarkably different from any woman you've dealt with so far. They place an *extremely* high value on family and family integrity. It's part of their culture. This is in marked contrast to what is happening in American society today as it relates to attitudes about marriage and family. In America, family life is subordinate to an individual's *"career"*. American women, Black and white, in increasing numbers consider the vocation of being a housewife and mother repulsive.

Family ties and links to your ancestors are extremely important in Asian culture. Relationships are not taken lightly. In their cultures there is no casual, cavalier dating like Americans engage in. Women just don't sample the waters to see which man has the best sex technique before they marry him. A very close and dear female friend of mine remarked to me several years ago,

> *"..why I just would not dream of marrying a man before I tested him out sexually. We may not be compatible there."*

I think her experiences since then, have mitigated that view somewhat. She dated a few men after having said this. Each one was a total and complete fool. Sex may have been good, but a fool is a fool is a fool. Many a woman has been murdered by the same man who screwed them good. Her attitude is not common with Philippine women. Philippine women are very old fashion about this. Don't misunderstand me. They are not prudes. Sexually, they are as fulfilling as any girl you could ever meet. Their aim is to please you. It's just not socially accepted in their culture to *'sample the sexual waters'* before you leap. Once she is married however, her sexual creativity will amaze you. I had one American girl tell me that she never cared at all if the men she was sexually involved with enjoyed the experience or not. Her thing was;

> *"...I got mine, did you get yours? Too bad if you didn't. You have to get out now bro. I got other things to do."*

Men who have returned from Thailand report it to be sexual heaven. Thai women are also unbelievably pretty. The 'sexual heaven' comments refer to the Thai *'ladies of pleasure'*. If you're in the habit of engaging the services of a prostitute, Thai prostitutes qualify as the best in the world. But I should ope that right now this is not the area of your interest. The Thai woman likely to be a candidate for your attention will be lovely, demure, brown and inventive sexually. The Kama Sutra, that well know picturesque manual of sex, did not originate in India as many people assume. It originated in Thailand. As an aside, don't pass up a chance to see Thai dancers. They are the most unbelievably esoteric and divine performers you can possible imagine.

When an Asian lady begins to accept your company it's because she has accepted you as a probable husband. Before she gets to this point in her thinking, she will have evaluated YOU carefully. Put yourself in her shoes. You're going to be asking her to come thousands of miles away from her family, homeland, and her ancestral burial grounds. She will probably be here with little or no contact from people of her own country. She'll feel like a stranger in a strange place because that is precisely what she'll be. You will be her only source of comfort and security. The degree of difference between the American culture and her native culture will cause her to go into an emotional shock. It may take her a very long time to adjust to American life.

Shortly after my wife arrived in America she was exposed to vomit directly on a MAC machine keyboard, as well as a pile of human turds in the lobby of Wanamakers department store in Philadelphia. All this occurred within a short three hour time span. The following week she had the grand opportunity to see more human turds lying at the top of an exit from the Broad Street Subway leading into the City Hall courtyard. Can you imagine it? The seat of city government was pointed to by a stack of human shit! My wife's first few months in America were very stressful. She witnessed the many mental defectives roaming the city streets talking to themselves and engaged in all their bizarre behavior. You and I are in the habit of ignoring these occurrences but your new lady will be shocked. Some of these weirdos are so bizarre that they shock those of us who have lived here for most of our lives. Now imagine if we see a nut in the street who shocks US, consider just how much of a shock it is to your new bride. I once saw this white mental defective on downtown Chestnut street grabbing women by the shoulders, putting his head down about their navel and then looking back up at them while his head was still down there. He'd say "but Miss, I can't breath properly!". He'd hold this position for a few seconds then move on to the next woman and repeat this strange ritual. There were two cops on the corner watching him. They didn't move a muscle to help anybody. The poor women were petrified. Imagine if this guy did this to your new bride soon after she arrived in the country. She might not survive the experience. Your lady would never in her wildest imagination think that waiting for her is some human crap on the sidewalks of an American street or some wackout acting and talking like a fool. Her anxiety, as I've already mentioned, has a lot to do with her leaving her family and going *anywhere* far from them. The strange things she'll see in America will justify her fears. Since she will be in your hands during these stressful times for her, she must be certain that your intentions are honorable and that you are a man of the greatest integrity before she feels she can trust ad commit herself to you.

You will discover that your Asian lady has one primary objective. It's to please you. She is very accommodating and will do all she can to make you feel comfortable. She will always be polite and demure. She will reinforce in you the notion that you are the '*king of the castle*'. This is in marked contrast to the American Black girl who doesn't know what the word polite means and could give a dam wether you're comfortable or not. Believe you me, before the American Black woman sees you as the king of the castle, frogs will start crapping corn flakes. If you should marry an Asian lady you will discover that you will still have the **characteristic #1**[28] problems, *BUT* it will be much easier to deal with them. Your Asian wife comes from a more disciplined culture. This helps her do a better job of controlling the negative side of feminine emotionalism. When a disagreement breaks out, assuming you are in the right, she has the ability to reel back in and accept the fact that you are right and then make a change. Sometimes she may not say to you "I'm Sorry" in a direct way, but she'll say it indirectly. She'll do it in a way consistent with the idea of saving face. She

[28] See Chapter Three

might bake you your special carrot cake or bean pie. She might
even get up the stomach to cook you some hog maws or
chitlings. She may venture out and buy you a special present
or something of that nature. No matter how she does it, she will
be determined to apologize to you and make amends. You have
to let her save face. Saving face is very important component
of Asian culture. You are expected to let a person save face. Not
to do so is considered a sign of barbarism. You will have to learn
the art of indirect communications. It's the oriental style to be
subtle and indirect. Americans pride themselves in *"letting it
all hang out"* and *"letting the anger show"*. Your Asian wife,
particularly in the beginning, is not likely to be this way. She
comes from a society in which outward displays of emotions
are frowned upon. She will tend to keep her anger within. You
have to encourage her to talk about areas of your relationship
she may not be too happy about. She may never tell you. She'll
just endure it. In general, disagreements are resolved because
of her willingness to accept the fact that she may be wrong. You
too must accept the fact that you are wrong whenever you are.
Your American girl is reluctant to do this. She's right when
she's right and right when she's wrong. When she knows she's
in the wrong, the miserable D.O.B. just won't admit it. She's
not a good mother image for your children.

    Asian women are well known for their sense of duty,
loyalty and responsibility. These are characteristics that
American Black women either don't now anything about or
find repulsive. You won't have to ask your Asian wife to cook
dinner or do the laundry or clean house. These are things she
does automatically, with no sense of burden. You'll probably
have to stop her from working too hard. I had this problem.
When my wife arrived here, she immediately went into working
gear. Every time I turned around she was cooking or cleaning
or doing something. I had to take her by the arm and sit her
down and make her rest. I never really succeeded in keeping
her down for long. In her mind, it was unthinkable that she
should rest while there was work to be done. I was feeling guilty
because of how hard she was working. I'd try to chip in and help
but she wouldn't have it. (Actually I think she thought I just
made more of a mess when I tried to help). She's very thrifty and

knows how to make a dollar stretch. The meals she cooks will be rather interesting to say the least. It may take some getting used to, and some compromise on both your parts to deal with this change in your cuisine. They have a diet radically different from what we are used to. Appreciate her cooking though, it's probably a healthier style of cooking than what you've been used to.

You won't have to argue about whether to "go to the movies or go to the game". She'll go where you want to go. You'll have to get used to this. In other words, you actually have to get used to being treated good by a woman and treated with respect. If my wife and I planned to go out to dinner or to the movies, by habit I would ask her where she wanted to go and what she wanted to see. I had been conditioned to think that this was being courteous. My wife would invariably tell me that we were to go where *I* wanted to go. This was no 'put on'. She expected the *captain of the ship* to set the course. It was my sudden obligation to be captain.

One of the more common mistakes American men make when communicating with an Asian lady is to bring up the topic of sex so soon after you make an introduction. Gentlemen, don't even joke about sex! I'm sure your mind is not so small that you can't come up with a host of other topics to discuss first. You can be reasonably certain that the lady of your interest has had no prior interactions with men other than the men in her family and those she may interact with at school or on her job if she works. It is unlikely that your lady will have had any sexual experience no matter what her age is, if she's never been married. We're used to dealing with these women here in America who have a totally different attitude towards sex and sexual relations than the women from the Philippines. If you're dealing with a lady from Thailand, I'm told you can feel a bit more free to bring up the topic of sex rather early in your 'relationship' but I wouldn't advise it. There's plenty of time to talk about sex. Don't rush things. Get to know her first. Let her get to know you. Men I know who have traveled to West Africa report that the sexual morays there are not entirely different from those here in America. It is a bit more permissible to talk about, and engage in, sex early in the

:lationship. This is not in general true with Asian women. ›emember, what I'm saying does not apply to Asian women ho "service" GI's while stationed over there.

You will probably notice two primary 'looks' Philippine women have. One is a very Oriental facial structure, the ◖ther is a slightly more Western structure. Those of the latter ⁄pe are still clearly identifiable as Asian, but they don't have ◖ach things as the pointed eyes for example, so typical of the ◖hinese look. They also may be a bit taller than usual for ◖sians.

Your Asian lady is very intelligent. She will be watchⁿg you with a very critical eye. She will be evaluating your ◖orrespondence carefully. She will take note of what you say, ⁄hen you say it, and how you say it. She is quick to notice ◖nything that appears tricky. When you start writing to her, ◖on't try any of your slick Black stuff. It won't work. As a ◖ractical matter, she probably won't even understand the ◖pecific language of it. If you've gotten this far in the book, you ◖hould be the type of man who will have already decided to ◖bandon his old Mr. Slick ways. Be straight forward and ◖onest. Do yourself and other Black men a favor and refrain ◖rom bringing your partner in the **New-Reconstruction** over ◖ere based upon some slick deception. She'll only report back ◖ her family and friends that you aren't worth a dam. This will ◖ake it tougher for other Black men who are honest and ◖esirous of developing relationships with Asian woman to ◖ccomplish this.

Your lady, if she is Philippine, probably speaks ◖nglish with varying degrees of proficiency. She will also speak ◖agalog, the national language, as well as the language of her ◖articular region. Many of them have a facility with Spanish. ◖n fact very many Philippine surnames are Spanish names. ◖his is because of the influence of Spain in the Philippines for ◖ couple centuries. It is EXTREMELY important that you use ⁄ery simple sentences and words. You'd be surprised just how ◖uch your language is interlaced with local slang phrases and ◖erms. What you will discover is your English is not so much English as it is "Americanese". Your lady's instruction in English was probably conducted using the British form of

English or Standard English as it is called. The American form of English is very different from Standard English and may not so easily understood by your lady. Your colloquial American English is sure to cause confusion, misunderstanding, and sometimes anger. Most guys I know who were writing foreign women report that the relationships they were developing collapsed at least one time because of misunderstandings arising from language problems. I once greeted an Asian lady with *"what's up"*. All I got back from her was silence. The phrase made no sense to her at all. She took it as a literal request on my part, for her to tell me what was **up in the sky** above her head. On another occasion I said to a lady from Ghana, *"how you doing"*. Again there was confusion. She politely responded with *"How am I doing what sir?"*. If I didn't know any better, I may have thought she was being a smart mouth. However, it quickly occurred to me that my 'greeting' had caused some confusion and had motivated her to say to herself;

> *"I wonder why he is asking me to tell him how I am performing some sort of task. I'm not performing any task right now".*

Keep your language plain and simple. Use more words if you must, but strip slang and provincial dialect out of your speech. As an example, supposed you would ordinarily say;
> "I could never have accomplished such a difficult task alone."

It would be better to say it like this instead;
> "I did not want to do the work by myself. It was too hard. My friends helped me."

This approach will avoid the misunderstandings bound to occur with more complex speech patterns. Of course if she speaks excellent English or you speak excellent Tagalog, then you can disregard the above advice. There was a study conducted through the University of Washington in 1990 by Dr. Jeanne Lin which reported that the major cause of tension and dissatisfaction that existed between Intercultural couples could be traced to the problems arising from language, that is, the couples not having a firm grasp of the nuances of each other's language. Dr. Lin reported that the results of her survey indicated a very high level of marital satisfaction between the couples even though the tension levels tended to be higher than those in the general population. Again the tension levels could be traced in large part to the problem of language.

For those of you who do not plan to make a personal visit to the lady's native country (I never did either), correspondence and phone calls will be the mainstay of your communications. Keep a good record of all these calls as you will eventually have to demonstrate to Immigration officials that you have been communicating with your intended spouse for an appreciable period of time. INS (Immigration and Naturalization Service tries to protect you from what they call *"convenience marriages"*. These are marriages made quickly by a foreign national and an American because the foreign national's only objective is to enter the U.S. This is, as a general rule, a situation not in your best interest. Being able to show telephone logs and letters that have accrued over a long period of time evidences the sincerity of the foreign national.

Usually the lady you are writing will put pressure on you right away for a picture. Don't give it to her. Make her wait. take a few months to feel her out by her letters. Her words will be unencumbered by the distraction of having seen you. the written correspondence will be a better judge of the state of her heart. You'll probably be writing to more than one person at first. Soon you'll feel compelled to narrow it down to one or two ladies. Don't get discouraged if you don't hear from the lady for several months. Many countries over there have terrible postal departments. In addition, the area is subject to such natural disasters as monsoon rains, hurricanes, and volcano eruptions. The roads over there are not too good and these disasters make such matters like mail delivery impossible. In addition, the US postal system is not necessarily the best. One letter I

---

29   Marital Satisfaction And Conflict In Intercultural Marriages, Jeanne L. Lin, Ph.D. Univ, of Washington, Seattle, WA. The study was conducted by interviewing 214 Asian women and 240 American men over a period of 11 months. Couples were contacted from client list of 5 agencies similar to the AAWS.

sent to my wife when she was in Hong Kong, arrived four months after I sent it. It had been sent to Korea in error. It sat there for months then was returned to me. This is typical. Telephone service can be equally troublesome. If you're writing to someone in West Africa, you can just about forget getting through to them on the phone. Even if you do, you stand an excellent chance of having the call disconnected by some fluke in the phone system of that country.

If the lady you're writing to suddenly starts talking about matters dealing with her expenses or her family's expenses, go on the alert. Watch out if she begins to talk about how expensive her little brother's school supplies are for example. She's setting you up for the big *hand in your pocket* game. This is probably a big city girl who has had some contact with the GI's. She may be the kind of person who just wants to get your cash, get to America here, and then leave you. This does happen on occasion. Your foreign lady is infinitely better than your American one, but I'm not alleging that all foreign women are saints. If you've been introduced to an Asian lady via one of the *"pen pal"* agencies here in America, you have to be careful. Not all of them are reputable. One of the most reputable and reliable of the agencies is located in Orcutt California. [30] It is operated by Mrs. Tesse Florence. Mrs. Florence is always extremely helpful and is an expert when it comes to communicating with and brining an Asian (particularly Philippine) lady to America. There are other agencies you ay consult but my best advice to you is to consult with Mrs. Florence at AAWS first. If you read the footnotes you'll see her agencies mailing address and phone number. If you are availing yourself of the services of these agencies take a good look at their brochures showing pictures of the ladies. If the pictures show asses and tits, low cut blouses, sexy smiles, legs

[30]   Asian American Worldwide Services P.O. Box 2777, Orcutt California, 93455; (805) 937-5230. Other agencies include Cherry Blossoms in Kapaau Hawaii; Orchid Pen Pal Club in Los Angeles; Asian Wives in San Francisco, and Asia West Connections in Los Angeles. I have found that the more conservative ladies are sponsored by AAWS. The least conservative, sponsored by Cherry Blossoms. The other agencies sponsor ladies that are somewhere in between AAWS and Cherry Blossoms.

wrapped around poles, G-strings, etc., avoid that agency. It's not reputable as far as I'm concerned. These may be city girls who have already been screwing the troops. If you want a *legs around the pole* girl, you don't have to go to the other side of the world to get one. You can accomplish this within 5 minutes of your house. I'm sure that there are men who may not have the same interpretation of the girls in these brochures that I have, and I concede that I have no information suggesting that these girls experience a higher divorce rate. My personal feeling is that in view of what we have experienced here in America, why take a chance at the possibility of problems when you don't have to. If there is the slightest indication of a potential problem don't go ahead with that girl or agency. Deal with a more conservative agency with more conservative women. Some of the Black men who have availed themselves of agency services permit the agency to furnish their names to other prospective clients. Contacting these brothers is one of the best ways to get some of your concerns addressed. You'll hear first hand, of the experiences these men are having married to a foreign national. When I called a few of these men, I heard nothing but praises of the women they had married. They were frank and honest in telling me also of a few problems that had arisen but when they compared their overall experiences with their Asian brides against their experiences with these American spear chukkers, the general feeling was that they wouldn't trade their Asian bride for anything in the world.

I've noticed that certain Asian cultures are rather indulgent when it comes to raising their male children. I watched Cambodian and Laotian (the Mung people in Laos) school children playing during recess. The boys kept giving the girls karate kicks and girls rarely, if ever, retaliated. Mothers would watch and rebuke a girl child if she struck back. I asked some of the teachers if this was normal and was told that it was. Boy children were considered special while girl children were considered less valuable. Historically, in Asia, this has been the view, but I was not aware that what amounted to abuse was tolerated to the extent that I saw it. My wife is a bit too indulgent with our children. I'm not yet certain that this is the result of her personal tendency or if it is cultural. It has caused a problem but being the accommodating person she is, she's learning to adjust to a different approach to child raising. Were she an American Black girl, she'd resist my attempts to instruct her in the proper disciplining of a child. One of the worse combinations is a Black woman and a male child particularly if she's a single parent. You want to increase the odds that a boy child will have a totally screwed up head, let him be raised by a single, hostile, man hating Black woman. In general your Asian wife, with her tremendous sense of family and duty, will make a marvelous mother to the children.

AFRICAN LADIES

Over the course of many years, I have had the opportunity to meet many African women here in America and abroad. However I'll use, for my comments, some fresh information I've received from a few Black men who have returned from visits to West, East, and Northern Africa within the past year or two (1990-1992).

My observation of African women I've met here in the States is consistent with what men who have traveled to the region tell me. For the most part their natures are similar to Asian women. There are however a few distinctions. The first is that they are not as patient as Asian women. The men I know who had met women while they were in Africa, maintained a communications with them upon returning. Where the man gave a hint that he was interested in marriage, the women began to pressure him into decisive action. They wanted a proposal and they didn't want to wait too long. An Asian woman may communicate with you for two and three years, maintaining an exclusive contact with you and you alone and not pressure you for marriage. They'll give you ample time to be certain this is what you want to do. African women don't seem wiling to wait that long.

Each of the men I've talked to said almost the identical words;

"Man, I'll tell you, every Black man should visit the

continent. He has no idea of how much respect and courtesy he'll get over there. You have no idea what it's like to be in a place where everything good and bad is run by Black people. They're in charge. The women are incredible. They're so friendly. They're not hostile. They won't let you do things like cook or clean. They feel compelled to do it."

I met a man and woman from the West African country of Sierra Leone over a friend's house for dinner one evening. There was also an American Black girl present. She was a house guest of the host and had been there for roughly two weeks. My friend, a Black man, cooked and served dinner. After all of us ate a delicious dinner, he began to clear the table. At this point, the woman from Sierra Leone couldn't take it anymore. She kept insisting that SHE clean up and help. My friend respectfully declined her offer to help. The house guest got bored and went upstairs. The African woman looked at me with a shocked expression her face. She said,

"Its unbelievable. I don't understand it. How come that girl didn't clean up. How come she didn't cook the meal. I don't understand these American women. How come she left and went upstairs. These women here are so disrespectful!"

I laughed and told her that it would take the next week of evenings to explain the whole thing to her but that "This was the grand old USA". Latter on in the evening the African woman and I talked about child raising. She again expressed shock when I told her that I had raised my first son as a single parent for the first eight years of his life. She said that in her country that would have been impossible. If any woman saw you raising a child by yourself, they would immediately step in and offer to help you. They would offer themselves as governess or wife. At the very least, I would always have constant baby sitters. A man was suppose to be free to think and create. Child care was the responsibility of the woman and any woman who did not rally to a man with a child was a disgrace in her eyes.

Again I laughed and said "Welcome to America."

I know a few men who have sent African women considerable amounts of money by African standards. This money was usually sent to women who were given instructions to purchase various goods at the market places. The purchased goods were to be shipped back to America for resale. In each case there was a concern that the woman they sent the money to would keep it and vanish, or send you a few things and tell you that that's all she could buy with the money you sent. In each case, the fears of these gentlemen turned out to be unfounded. Goods were purchased and promptly shipped back. A latter audit showed that the money was spent properly. The women were honest. Now can you imagine sending an African man sending a Black American girl some cash under the same conditions. What do you think the American girl wold do with the cash? The only way that man would see the fruits of the money would be in the form of a picture of the American girl in that new gown she wore to the Kappa ball and that new jewelry she wore. That's where the money would go. Are you with me gentlemen? Can I get an Amen?

One interesting aspect of African culture is the institution of polygamy. It is not uncommon at all for a man to have more than one wife if he can support them. "Support" is a key word here. In Africa, the man carries the whole ball of wax, no *if's, and's* or *but's*. You are expected, without question, without protest, to furnish the woman with what she needs in the way of money or anything else. This notion of *"hey baby let's you and me get together and share expenses"* is a foreign notion to the African woman. It's definitely got to be *"excuse me sugar daddy, I need $50.00 for the so and so"*. The only acceptable response from you is **"here baby"**. This may sound at first like a greedy American girl. NO! The African woman sees you as the king, as the source of everything good. You are the source of her wisdom, of her protection, and her care. It's within this framework that her expectations of are formed. She is also thrifty and judicious in her use of money. If she asked for the $50.00, you can trust that's precisely what she needs. Your Black American girl would ask you for the $50.00 when all she needed was $1.25 for Jiffy mix. She'd pocket the rest and tell you that some home boy snatched the other $48.75 of groceries as she was coming back home.

There is an issue of color in Africa. I'm told that if a person is of mixed blood, he is likely to have a higher social status because of his lighter skin color. The problem is not as acute in Africa as it is in America however because there are so few Africans who are light. Therefore you don't notice this as an appreciable problem and you don't have millions of Black Africans wishing they were white. As an interesting aside, I once had an old man say to me;

"You ever wonder why Black people can always spot an African in the crowd. I mean you can have 20,000 Blacks at the stadium and yet you'll be able to pick out the African in the bunch. You've got 40 million Black people in America and not a dammed one of them looks African."

I hadn't thought of that before. People I know who have been to Nigeria and other places on the West coast of Africa report that even though they were brown, the Africans thought they were white. One friend of mine was referred to as a **Brown White Man**. This is because American Black people have European features. In essence, we look like sun tanned white people to a great many folks in the world. However, this does not hold you up in Africa and if anything it gives you an edge. African women consider the look of the American Black man handsome. One African woman told me that in the American Black man, she saw the best of both worlds, white and Black. She got blackness of soul and whiteness in features. I had mixed feelings when I heard her. It suggested to me that there was on some level at least a vestige of identity crises within her. Beauty to her meant European features. In her mind, American Black men were 'beautiful' because they had white features. There seems to be a correlation between identity crises in Black areas of the world, and who the old colonial power was. Those Black countries who were under British control tend to have the greater problems with their identity as Black peoples. It seems that the Americans learned their racial hatred tricks from the British who always viewed their brown or Black colonial subjects as subhuman. This is an attitude distinct from other former European colonial powers. You should access this as you select the county where you'll be looking for your African bride. In all fairness, I don't get the impression that this identity crises is severe or that it presents you with any great problems. In other words I have no information which indicates that African women marry with an issue of skin color in mind. All evidence points to African women being humble, co-operative, loyal and dutiful.

If you are in Africa, you will discover that sexual customs are somewhat similar to here in that here is little prohibition to premarital sex. Women who are not married expect that they will be asked to have sex with their employers for example. I'm not suggesting this is rampant, but it would not shock a women if she were so propositioned. Men who are hosting other men will often offer you a woman for sexual pleasure. This may seem like abuse by standards here, but in many place is Africa it is merely the accepted custom by both men and women. I'm told however that once a woman is married, all this stops. I've spoken to many brothers who have concerns about the issue of virginity and their potential spouses. I think it's wise for you to question as many men as you can touch base with who have married African women so you can get a firm handle on this issue if it concerns you.

The cautions I mentioned earlier about language apply when it comes to African women. Remember that most people in the world who are trained in the English language, are trained in Standard English, that is, the English of the British Isles. As I said before, the American form of English is very different in many respects from standard English. Your potential African wife may have a difficult time understanding some of the words and phrases you may be using.

I watched a few men try to hook up with women from Northern Africa, in particular from Egypt. In the cases I am aware of, the relationships never got past a very casual friendship. Each of the women demonstrated an anxiety about coming to a Christian country. They were very much concerned about leaving their families. They had preconceived ideas about the nature of American men. American men have the reputation of being insincere playboys who think they can buy any women in the world. One young Black man I know who was writing to an Egyptian girl, sent her gifts in the form of two checks for $50.00 on two different occasions. He was interested in the girl but for his own legitimate reasons, did not want to commit himself to marriage to her at that time. I suggested to him that this girl was not going to wait forever, for him to propose marriage. His response was that she *would* wait and that the money he was sending would "cool her out" and keep her under *his* time frame. He thought he could buy her patience. The girl cashed the first check but never cashed the second. Months after receiving his second check, she sent it back to him with a letter letting him know that marriage to him was not in the cards. He finally had to admit that money could not buy everything, all the time. Such a view he had adopted from white people. I'm sure you can find American men who have married Egyptian women. I doubt if you can find too many of them. I doubt if you can find more than a few Black men who have taken this route. I think the cultural gap is far too great to bridge at this point in time. I don't recommend it unless you plan on moving to Egypt, becoming a devout Muslim, marrying there, and staying there.

Women from West and East Africa are very interested in getting to the West. They are very receptive to marrying an American. There are reports that women of the South Eastern part of Africa, in particular Swaziland, Botswana, Zimbabwe and Madagascar, tend to look a trifle more like Blacks here in America because of the supposed higher incidence of mixing of the races. I think that American Black men are more inclined to see these women as attractive. I've been cautioned however that the dominance of the white minority in the south has resulted in a fair amount of self-esteem problems with some of the indigenous peoples. I don't believe this is a really big problem. The main issue is wether the woman will make you a good wife if you are a good husband. If she will take proper care of the house and children, if she is pleasant and loyal, respectful and industrious, any lack of esteem will hopefully ebb away as a result of association with you. After all, by the time you get to the point in which you're ready to take on a non American national as a wife, you've already shown yourself to be a cut above average, and a man with a healthy sense of self-esteem. It'll rub off on her if this needs to occur. Her years long conditioning in favor of responding positively to male guidance and instructions mitigates in favor of believing that once you discuss any issue of esteem with her, she'll make an extra effort to resolve this problem. She'll probably be successful in her efforts. She'll understand how unhappy you are with this aspect of her personality and how detrimental it may be to the children. Remember, these women, unlike what you've been used to dealing with, don't resist your good sense ideas and policies.

What seems to be the significant difference between an Asian woman and African woman? The first difference is obvious. The two groups look different. Next there is a difference in patience between the two. African woman are a trifle less patient than Asian women but this difference is for all practical purposes no barrier to a happy and successful marriage. The odds that the African woman is a virgin are slightly less than those odds for an Asian. This may or may not be a problem for you depending on your own guidelines. What would make a man choose one over the other? Men I have discussed this question with, and who show a strong preference for an African women are men who feel it absolutely necessary not to break away from the race, that is to replace the American Black woman with another <u>Black</u> woman. These men are operating more within a political framework than men who may choose an Asian route. There are of course men who choose Spanish women from any of the Latin American countries. We'll touch on this a bit latter.

Those of you who can afford the air fare, are well served by a visit to Africa. Your best bet is to acquaint yourself with some Africans living in your city, letting them know of your plans to visit their country. You want to have them, on your behalf, secure you living quarters. Many families would love the opportunity to host you by renting you living space in their house. In Sierra Leone for example you can pay a family $10.00 to $15.00 US dollars a week to stay there and another

$1.00 per day for a girl to come by and do the cooking and cleaning. The $10.00 is probably more that family makes in a month. Of course I'm not saying that each and every house charges this but according to my sources who have recently come back from the area, this would be the typical arrangement.

If you plan on going to the country of Nigeria, you'd had better be on your guard. The level of corruption there is high. They have something called "Bashee". This amounts to extortion money. If you're a foreigner, particularly American, officials everywhere you go, confront you for Bashee. If you want to proceed along the road, pay some Bashee and the police officer will let you pass. If you want to get through customs, pay some Bashee and you'll make it, otherwise you're in for a delay. I know travelers who never had this experience there, but I know more who did. One friend of mine played it smart. He wrote letters to the head of the police advising him in advance that he was coming. With the help of a Sierra Leone citizen, it was arranged that the Chief of Police meet my friend at the airport and protect him all the way through the entry process. My friend had no problems at all. When word got out that he was under the protection of the Police Chief, we got treated well and considered himself relatively safe from extortionist. It's good practice wherever you go, to identify yourself as traveling for investment purposes. Touch base with the higher ups. They'll make sure you're given the VIP treatment. Remember, you're the *"Brown White Man"* from America. It's assumed that you're rich. By their standards you **are** rich. High officials are pleased to have the opportunity to make a few bucks by serving your interest while you're a guest in their country.

Having established a friendship with an African who is already here in America can be very valuable as I indicated earlier. If you can find one who is willing to return home for a while, he can assist you by screening out undesirable women and introducing you to acceptable prospects. The word will get out that you are there and many women will want to meet you. You'll be treated like royalty. Remember don't be discouraged by those who tell you they were treated like shit. They probably stayed in the tourist areas, looked like tourist and got ripped off as happens to tourist. You're going to be traveling a bit differently. You'll be protected by officials and "living with the people". You'll not be considered a naive tourist.

BRIEF WORD ON CARIBBEAN WOMEN

What's my brief word on the Caribbean woman? *BE EXTREMELY CAREFUL. THE RED FLAG IS UP!.* When you consider a woman from the "Islands" you run the risk of playing with fire. Let me explain. Don't even think of dealing with one them who is already in America. They are usually a little more than an American girl with an accent. They're extremely aggressive and very materialistic. They can be just as flippant with their mouths as the American girls. The majority of men I know who have married them or have dated them, are under a constant pressure to satisfy their high materialistic standards. What I am saying is more true with the Jamaican women and less true with women from Trinidad or women from Barbados. In Barbados skin color can be rather important. The lighter you are, the more breaks you get. Barbados is sometimes referred to by other islanders as the land of snobs or the intellectual island. Sometimes they can be more British than the British. They have an intense national pride and are proud of themselves as a Black nation but they wear the legacy of British rule. Some cousins of mine hosted a young lady form Barbados a few summers ago. When she met me, I'm told she went berserk. She was really into what she considered my light skin color. I took a look at myself in the mirror and got a bit confused. I looked brown to me, but to her I was light and desirable. This and this alone was her criterion for evaluating me. Each time I call the island and speak to family or others, I get the conversation going in the direction of skin color. The women all show a preference for 'fair' skin as they call it. Gentlemen, wether you are light or dark, you don't need this sort of thing. You're trying to cast off Black women who have been victimized by their experience in the Western hemisphere. You're going East with the expectations that you will come across Black and brown people less negatively affected by white domination. In the Virgin Islands, St. Croix to be exact, I once received help from a girl who was working in St. Croix but was a native of thee island of Antigua. She was giving me help in procuring Reggae' records. I offered to treat her to lunch to show my appreciation. She accepted and asked me where we were going to eat. I told her we'd have lunch at the "Cafe' Francais". She immediately freaked out and broke into a sweat. She said she couldn't eat there because white people went there. At first I thought she was a Black nationalist who felt it beneath her sense of revolutionary pride to fraternize with white folks. All the places she wanted to go to were closed so we wound up at the Cafe'. When we entered I noticed she kept her head bowed low. I thought she was wanted by the local police for radical activity and was hiding her face. We sat down and next to our table was a young white couple from Florida. The girl was plastered. When she heard my American accent, she got up from her table, came over to me and sat on my lap. The girl I was with put her head down on the table and kept looking around. Later I found out what the deal was. She though the police were going to come lynch me and her for having contact with a white person. She was afraid of them. She had spend her whole life feeling inferior to and being afraid of whites. The fact that I was actually touching a white person was too much for her to bear. After I left St. Croix, I received a letter from her in which she offered to come up to the U.S. and "stay by me", that is live with me and marry me. Needless to say I declined the offer. This girl was too slaved whipped for my taste. I figured she might to go down town and after seeing all the mixed couples walking around, have a heart attack. I'd wind up having to pay the funeral expenses for a slave-head Negress. This just wouldn't do! I'm not wasting my time or resources on Western Black women with "anti Black man" sentiments or slave mentalities.

If you're not talking about Barbados or Trinidad and perhaps a few other islands I'll mention, there's a good chance that you talking problems. I'm sure you'll find many relationships between American Black men and Caribbean women that are functional, but I always say play the betting man. Play the odds. Where there's a history of problems, avoid them. You go walking into a relationship with a Jamaican woman for example, you run a great risk of having problems. As I said they've a high incidence of aggressiveness and all the other corruptions common to an Americanized woman. If we're discussing options, we're discussing them from the point of view of final victory, that is victory in the context of the message of this book, victory from the negative influence of whites. You make a backwards run when you take on one of the very people who shows signs of victimization. If you make such a choice, you might as well never have started on the road to victory. You might as well never have read this book. If you want to get a handle on the nature of Caribbean women here in Philadelphia, there are a few clubs where they frequent. Visit a few and study the women. One Caribbean club is well noted for the way the women dance. You might as well be in bed with them. Now, you may find it enjoyable to attend the club, but whatever she's doing with you, she's been doing with every other man who danced with her. You want her for a wife? But if you're not a Doctor, Lawyer or Indian Chief, or if you don't have a luxury car, skip over that part of the index. I have met women from the Caribbean country of Dominica. They were lovely, intelligent and humble. They didn't have that aggressive nature. They weren't as materialistic as other islanders. Women from Panama were also pretty and demure. I found them charming beyond reproach. They're another group of women worthy of your attention.

In brief, unless you are very knowledgeable of the Caribbean area, and have a basis for assessing on which island the women tend to be the sort of humble sweet person you're looking for, the odds are that you'll get that aggressive, materialistic, stubborn Caribbean woman who wants you to work nine jobs for the sole purpose of buying her that Jaguar she's seen on the Jamaican neighborhood TV screen.

LATIN AMERICA
Some of the most endearing and beautiful women of

the world are found in Latin America. They have a strong sense of family. They are hard workers and very loyal. They're also rather jealous and possessive. They tend to be rather temperamental however, hot tempered is the usual term. I personally have not experienced this supposed side of their personality but other men always speak of it. The women of Brazil are among the most desirable women in the entire world. Their beauty is beyond belief. They also are good workers and have a strong sense of family. The overall economic situation in the country has been depressed for ages. The result is that the women have not had the opportunity to develop a highly materialistic nature. The simple things of life impress them. The capacity to have one or two nice dresses is adequate. In practical terms, this simplistic approach to materialism translates into couples spending more time evaluating and appreciating each other. If a woman's mind is always on that diamond ring she wants, it won't be on you! If her time and yours is spent preoccupied with acquiring every gadget imaginable, again, it won't be spent in quality family time. Many of the women from Brazil still do their laundry by hand. Such a woman is appreciative of clean water, detergent and a washing machine. She doesn't need a palace and every so called modern convenience in the world to feel like a whole woman. I know a fellow who dated exclusively, Latin American women with an emphasis on Brazilian and Nicaraguan women. It was paradise for him. As a point of interest, Brazilian women are expected to be virgins by the time they get married. Law and custom in Brazil is such that a man can send his wife away if he discovers she was not virgin. Brazil is rather tough about this. Men are actually allowed to kill their women if they're caught involved in an extramarital affair. The reports I get are that Brazilian men are rather hard on their women. The women appreciate the fact that you're not inclined to be brutal like their men. They'll love the fact that they are now living in affluent America with a man who does not take them for granted and who exhibits a compassionate nature. Gentlemen, the Brazilian woman is a sure bet. I've a friend who spends each summer in Brazil. He reports that he is able to live very well with relatively little US currency. he takes about 500

US dollars and lives like a Prince for the two months he's there. Of course if you're going like a typical tourist and living in the Holiday Inn you're going to pay stiff price. But if you're living with a family, or renting a room somewhere and you hire a lady to do your cooking, you can live well, while you research the area.

My primary objective in giving the overviews in this chapter was to encourage you to think beyond the boundaries of America. When I was going through problems with these American girls, I came to a point where I said to myself

"Man, everywhere you turn, no matter which one you deal with, they're a pain in the rear. Is this what life is like? Is this what's going to be the deal until I die?"

It never occurred to me that there were women elsewhere in the world who were not like these American girls. For years, I thought I was in a hopeless situation until, as I mentioned earlier in the book, I visited my friend who had married a Philippine lady and saw how different from what I was used to, his relationship was. For the first time I had hope. This chapter tries to give you hope. Shake yourself up and re-do your thinking. There are other women out there besides the American Black woman. They're waiting for you. You don't have to put up with nonsense. This was the point of the Options chapter. There isn't a single problem you're facing now with that American Black woman of yours that I haven't also faced. I did a switch. My wife is not an American Black woman. I no longer have problems. I spoke with a friend who conceded that Black men and women were in a state of war and that we had to struggle with them. I argued that it was not necessary to struggle with them, just get rid of them and get someone you don't have to struggle with. His approach to the problem we've ben talking about is not as straight forward as mine but he's slowly adopting my method. You can't argue with the facts. You can't argue with success. I had problems in the past, took a certain course of action, and now I don't have problems. This is the bottom line. I saw some white boys on a local talk show with their rebellious wives. One of the women was upset because her husband wouldn't let her hang out in bars and go to these Chippendale Boys strip shows. The talk show hostess right on the air told her that she knew her husband didn't allow this so she brought some male strippers on the show for the girl to see. In other words the hostess assisted the wives in mutiny against their husbands. When this show hostess did this I had to admit that she displayed what we Black lack, hard core comradeship. As far as that hostess was concerned, it was to hell with the desires and rules of a husband. Women had to rebel against heir husbands and they had to become comrades in support of each other's efforts to that end. The real tragedy as I have said all throughout this book that this comradeship and rebellion works because it goes unopposed by men.

One of the husbands on the panel told the audience,

"I am the big toe in my household. What I say goes. I am in charge, after me comes my wife then the kids. This is the way it has always been, it's the way it is now, and it's the way it's going to be always. If she doesn't like it, she can leave."

I said to myself "this white boy is right on target". He told the crowd that he didn't care one way or another what their sentiments were for or against him. His policy was his policy and that was all there was to it. The white boys have been getting some static from their women as a result of the women's movement and these boys are putting an end it. After I watched him I became rather disturbed as I thought about the Back men I know who are catching hell from their women but find all sorts of rationals *NOT* to take on that sort of direct position. Gentlemen, you don't have to put up with rebellious obnoxious Black women. Chose one from another country! This is direct revolutionary action. Take it and be happy!

THE LEGAL PROCESS

In order to bring your new lady into the country you have to go through a step by step Immigration process. At this point in time, the process is straightforward and simple. AAWS[31] does not recommend that you marry your fiance' in her native country. I concur. Doing this places her in an immigration status that is a bit more complicated to deal with. In addition, her local country's documentation requirements may make the process long and almost impossible. Foreigners in America all have what is called a VISA. A visa is a permit to travel to the country for specific purposes. Visa holders, depending upon which type visa they have, are allowed to work or not work, stay for a long time or only for a short time. Your lady will be coming here on what is called a **K1** Visa. This visa is for **Alien Fiancee's of American Citizens**. If you think you need help in going through the process, contact a local Immigration Attorney. You can also pay a small fee to AAWS and they will handle the whole thing for you. Let me caution you. I've come across a few men who want to bring their fiancee into the country using processes other than the K1 Visa process. Don't try it. One fellow I know married his lady after she arrived here on a visitors visa. She eventually had to leave the country, make application again under a visa specific for and spouses of U.S. citizens. This process took a very long time. She had to remain outside the country the entire time. Another fellow I knew married his fiancee in her own home country. It took him almost a year to complete the marriage because of the myriad of red tape her government put them through. In addition she had to be processed for the above visa. The K1 visa is the most straight forward way to go about this. It's specific for this task. you are well advised to follow the procedures for this visa and not skirt around them. You'll discover that your "short cuts" are in the final analysis, long cuts.

The first step for you is to fill out a form called **I-129FM PETITION FOR ALIEN FIANCE'(E).** You are the sponsor of your fiancee. It is you who petitions the Government to admit her and give her permanent status. Order the I-129FM form from your local Immigration Service. Consult your local Yellow Pages for the phone number you can call. INS will send you the form in the mail. Order the form by it's number not the title

---
[31] Asian American Worldwide Services, referenced earlier

of the form. The form ask you for your name and address, the name and address of your intended spouse, the address where the two of you intend to live while when she enters the country and under what circumstances did you meet. It is extremely important that you keep copies of all letters you send your future spouse. It is also important that you keep copies of your phone bills showing that you have called her. It is far better if you can arrange a personal meeting between the two of you. Technically, INS requires that the two of you have met face to face unless there is some compelling reason which precludes a face to face meeting. If you can show a very extended period of letter writing and phone calls, this will suffice in lieu of a face to face meeting. I'm talking about years of writing and phone calls. This policy of the INS is designed to protect the American citizen. You also have to fill and attach a form called **BIOGRAPHIC INFORMATION, G-325A.** You have to order two of these forms. Fill out one giving information about yourself. Send the other to your lady to fill out. Have her sign it and return it to you. It just ask for your addresses for the past five years and your employment for the same time period. Take a piece of paper as though you were writing a letter to the INS and just tell them that you are able to support your lady once she enters the country. Send them a copy of a blank check that you've voided out so they can see you have a checking account. Give them a rough idea of how much money is in the account and give them the name and address of your employer. Neither the employer or the bank is likely to be contacted. Get this letter notarized. It's then becomes a formal declaration that you represent yourself to be a person financially secure enough to support her for a period of 90 days. I'll explain this 90 day period in a minute.

When you complete the I-129F and enclose the application fee ($40.00), INS will notify the American Consular Officer in the place where the lady is residing. They will let her know they have received your petition on her behalf. They will request that she complete more forms and provide some additional information such as a local police report on her. Don't worry about this kind of thing. Your lady is not like people here. She wasn't doing any slick stuff so the police report will be blank. The information that is gathered by INS during this process is all on her, not on you. The focus is on her. Once she provides the U.S. Consular officer in her area with the information they need, she will be issued a K1 visa. There is a 90 day limitation on the visa. The time period starts from the time she enters the US borders, not from the time she is issued the visa. When she enters the U.S., have her get her Visa stamped with a Work Permission stamp just in case the two of you decide that she is to be employed after getting here. You must get married within 90 days of her entry into the country. Once the marriage takes place, you have up to two years to file the form **I-485, APPLICATION FOR PERMANENT RESIDENCE.** This form is a change of Status from her K1 visa to that of a **Permanent Resident.** You may have heard of the **"Green Card".** This is the card the Alien gets after their change of status from a Temporary Immigrant as in the case of your lady holding a K1 Visa, to a permanent resident. The application fee is $120.00 as of the writing of this chapter. As a permanent resident, your lady is absolutely in good shape. She's just about a citizen. In a few years, she'll be able to make formal application for citizenship which should be pro-forma approved.

CHAPTER-EIGHT

Integration Discarded: Liberty Gained

This chapter is only for those Black men who have by now decided, without reservation, that they want to cast off the chains of integrationist, dependency thinking, cultivate new and better relationships with New World Women and forge ahead with plans for the **New Reconstruction**. This chapter will provide you with some historical information designed to show you that it's possible to achieve independence. I want to make it clear to you that the purpose of this information is **not** to suggest that anybody should emigrate to Africa. It's to demonstrate that Black people who decide to co-operate with each other, work hard, and make the necessary sacrifices, can achieve independence and gain the respect of their women and children as well as the world at large. We will also study how it's possible for all of one's efforts to be undermined if a total and complete transformation of ones individual character and thought processes is not achieved. Some of the material in this chapter will be a repeat of things I have said earlier. It doesn't hurt however to re-enforce messages that encourage us to undergo a positive transformation of our natures.

We'll start our discussion with the premise that we desire liberty, prosperity, the respect of our women and children and of the world at large. If you didn't desire these things you wouldn't have gotten this far in the book. To maintain clarity throughout this discussion, let's be on one accord as to the meaning of the word Liberty. Liberty according to Webster's, is defined as *"Freedom"*. Freedom is then defined as *"the quality or state of being free*: **INDEPENDENCE"**. When we speak of liberty we must therefore be speaking in terms of independence from Euro-America with respect to matters of our basic subsistence, our defense and the justice we receive. Our present condition is such that our capacity to secure these things is far too much a function of the degree to which the Euro-Americans place or do not place obstacles in our path. In short, we are at the mercy of Euro-America. Money needed for our basic subsistence is given to us by being employed by a Euro-American company or by donations from the state treasury (welfare payments). Even our "independent street vendors" are at the mercy of Euro-Americans. A vendor who sells women's stockings sells a product manufactured by a Euro-American company. There are no African American owned industrial plants that synthesize the materials that go into the weaving of women's stockings. Such a vendor, though independent of Euro-Americans to a certain degree, depends on them to supply him with the goods he sells. The Euro-Americans, through their representatives, elected or appointed, regulate the quality and quantity of our food clothing and shelter. The defense of our women and children is in the hands of Euro-American administered police and military authorities. There are a few instances in which this may appear to be untrue, as in the case of the current Chairman of the Joint Chiefs of Staff. However, Black as he may be, he represents the interest of Euro-America. If it <u>were</u> in the interest of the **New Reconstruction** to establish friendly relations with an African country but <u>not</u> in the interest of Euro-America, the Black Chairman would defend the interest of Euro-Americans. As African Americans, we do not administer the judicial system. If we did, many African American men now in prison would not be there, and many who are there and shouldn't be, would be released. Under the **New Reconstruction Bureau of Justice**, the Rodney King verdict would have been an impossibility.

If it is true (and it is) that in matters of and defense and in matters of the quality and quantity of our food clothing and shelter, Euro-Americans dictate, then we are not experiencing liberty. If these matters were in our hands as African Americans we would be at the mercy of our own competence or lack thereof. We would be free to succeed or fail as a result of our own efforts. This would constitute a state of liberty. The American patriot who proclaimed "Give me Liberty or give me death"[32] understood that the condition of liberty is preferable to a condition of dependency arising from servitude. As African Americans we ought to be "captains of our own ship" rather

---

[32] Patrick Henry

than the wards and servants on the Euro-American's ship. We ought to be the regulators of our prosperity as opposed to being regulated. Liberty implies independence. Independence implies liberty. Dependence implies servitude. At this point in history we are at best, the servants of Euro-Americans, albeit unneeded servants, but servants with "auxiliary status" just the same.

If when comparing independence to dependence, we conclude that independence from Euro-Americans (liberty), is preferred to dependence (servitude), then a change is needed. The relationship between African Americans and Euro-Americans must be radically altered. The extent of this re-alteration will be revolutionary. It will be revolutionary because the current relationships between African Americans and the Euro-Americans will have to be utterly dissolved. Our future efforts must not take on the shape of mere rebellion, but of total revolution. The two are different. A rebellion does not seek to redefine social relations. It's objective is to replace the existing authorities with different authorities while maintaining the character of social relationships prior to the rebellion. Let us imagine for a minute living in a country with a king at the helm. If I should overthrow the king and make myself king, I have engaged in a rebellion. I did not alter the character of social relations. There was a king before the rebellion and in me there is yet still another king. Nothing has changed except the name of the king. But if I should dethrone the king, abolish monarchy and institute democracy, I will have utterly re-shaped the character of socio-political relations. In such an instance I will have been revolutionary. A revolution doesn't just replace existing authority with new authority but utterly destroys existing social relations in favor of a redefined relationship between the adversaries. Euro-Americans are our adversaries. As I have said, the present character of the relationship between African Americans and Euro-Americans is best described as we (African Americans) being their dependants. Such a relationship must be utterly re-shaped through a method that is revolutionary since our objective is to abolish and re-shape the existing dependency relationship. To further illustrate this let us assume another hypothetical. Let us assume that five minutes from now, on each residential block now occupied by African Americans, there is one person who owns a multi-billion dollar manufacturing establishment. Let us assume that these establishments employ all the people on each respective block. Let us assume that for every conceivable need the people have on each block an African American satisfies that need. From food to toilet paper, there is an African American owned and run manufacturing plant which satisfies these needs. If there should be a need for police services, there is an African American run police department functioning totally without the support of the Euro-American police structure. Under such conditions, we are independent of the Euro-American society. All of our needs are satisfied by us, through our own efforts, individually and collectively. Such a condition would constitute a revolutionary change in the character of relationships between ourselves and our adversaries, the Euro-Americans. The condition of African American dependence upon Euro-Americans for subsistence will have been abolished and a new relationship between the two racial groups will have been established. Dependence and servitude will have been replaced with independence and liberty. This is what I mean by revolutionary action as it relates to African Americans. It is to move from a condition of **"dependence on"** to one of **"independent of"** Euro-American socio-economic and defense structures. Once our revolutionary action produces liberty, we may find that a relationship with those on whom we formerly depended is useful. Such a relationship will have to be symbiotic.[33] It could not be permitted that such a relationship take on the characteristic of us being dependent on our former adversaries. This would be counter revolutionary.

The character of the relationships African Americans maintain with each other must be radically altered. The abolishing of dependency upon the Euro-Americans necessitates a dependency upon each other. I have said dependency implies servitude. Servitude in and of itself is not an evil. A dependency of African Americans upon each other is a serv -

---

[33]   Symbiosis refers to a condition in which two or more parties form a non-destructive relationship, mutually beneficial.

tude of sorts. But this is a healthy dependence. It is a healthy servitude. It is a servitude that seeks to advance each individual and the group as a whole. It's a post-revolutionary servitude. It differs from pre-revolutionary servitude in that it is not exploitive. It is symbiotic. It reflects team work. Contemporary African Americans, particularly those in urban areas, are not very skilled at interdependency and co-operation. This must change. Our failings in this area have been long standing and have been exploited by the Euro-Americans. In the 1920's Marcus Garvey commented on this problem,

> *"The Negro in Western civilization, because of his environments that force upon him a complex inferiority, is the most stubborn individual to discipline within the race. He has but little, if any, respect for internal racial authority. He cannot be depended upon to carry our an order given by a superior of his own race...This lack of obedience to orders and discipline checkmates the real, worthwhile progress of the race..."* [34]

I have already said that we must revolutionize the manner in which we relate to each other. We must also revolutionize our habits and attitudes. Presently we exhibit the social habits of a slave class, a class of people reed to serve a master. This must change. Those who fail to successfully conduct this "personal revolution", in which long standing anti-independence attitudes and habits are abolished will be an impediment to revolutionary progress. Any African-American socio-political revolution can not hope to succeed if it is torn from within its own ranks by divisiveness, bad habits and counter revolutionary thought patterns. Interpersonal relationships between man and woman, husband and wife, child and parent, supervisor and the supervised, will have to be radically altered from their present state. The present character of these interpersonal relationships bears the mark of the destructive influences of our adversaries. African American women, for the most part are in a state of rebellion against African American men. As men we have lost the full faith and

[34]   Philosophy and Opinions of Marcus Garvey, Vol.2 pp 292

confidence of our women. African American children are growing up without the zeal for independence, without a sense of purpose, without discipline, without fathers and all to often with weak mothers. They are rebelling against everything, aimlessly venting their frustrations against members of their own community. But if you've gotten this far in the book you are aware of this and are aware of the solutions to the relationship crises I have tendered.

In summary we can say that we must revolutionize the character of our relationship with the Euro-Americans and we must revolutionize the character of relationships amongst ourselves. In order to achieve this we must assume several burdens. We must assume them in the following order;

1. Reject the denial syndrome and develop revolutionary zeal.
2. Study our situation scientifically.
3. Devise the revolutionary alternatives.
4. Implement the revolutionary alternatives.
5. Defend the revolutionary achievements.

Let us discuss each of the above in turn.

REJECT THE DENIAL SYNDROME AND DEVELOP REVO-LUTIONARY ZEAL:
If we are not willing to accept the facts of our history and our present condition, we will never rise above our condition. If a man should say to himself that "things have gotten better", he speaks folly. The central question is *"are we more independent from the Euro-Americans today than we were yesterday"?* The answer is a resounding **NO**. Integrationist would have trouble answering that question since true independence was never and still is not their goal. However, to the question *"Are we better off today than we were yesterday?"*, the integrationist would answer with a resounding **YES**. Integrationist lack self esteem. They see their destiny intrinsically linked with Euro-Americans. Each time an integrationist is allowed to live next door to a Euro-American, others of them will claim that *"Today is better than yesterday. One more of us has been extended the privilege of Euro-*

American presence."

An African American who cherishes liberty, uses the word "we" to refer to himself and other African Americans. When an integrationist uses the word "we" he means himself and his Euro-American "friends" he thinks he has. To an integrationist it is inconceivable that he could do well on his own, that is, without reference to Euro-Americans. The integrationist can't imagine life without them. Such a thought is a horror to him. The integrationist defines prosperity as being permitted to live with, eat with, and socialize with Euro-Americans. It doesn't matter to him that he is beholding for every crumb on his table. As long as he can be a living manifestation of *"little and black boys and black girls who have been able to join hands with little white boys and white girls"*, if I may be allowed to paraphrase part of Dr. King's now infamous I Have a Dream speech. Such a man will say that he has *"overcome"*. This integrationist loves that part of the civil rights song that goes *"blacks and whites together, blacks and whites together someday..."* It doesn't matter to him that Euro-Americans have long since rejected integration. The African American integrationist will still push and push to be included where he is not wanted even it means assuming an inferior social station. The integrationist believes deep in his heart that it is far better to be a lowly servant to the Euro-Americans than a free man, albeit a struggling free man.

An unreformed integrationist is a threat to our revolutionary efforts. Marcus Garvey was a true lover of liberty. Integrationist were instrumental in bringing down Garvey. Several of them authored a letter to the then U.S. Attorney General which read in part,

"..As the chief law enforcement officer of the nation, we wish to call your attention to a heretofore unconsidered menace to harmonious race relationships. There are now in our midst certain Negro criminals and potential murderers, both foreign and American born, who are moved and actuated by intense hatred against the white race. These undesirables continually proclaim

that all white people are enemies of the Negro... [35]

The authors of this letter composed and forwarded it not upon solicitation but upon their own desire to assist the American government in destroying any Black man, American or otherwise, who loved liberty and was actively engaged in the effort to free African Americans from the death grip of their enemies. The signers named Garvey in particular as the arch enemy of integration. Integrationist, in their zeal, will conspire with your adversary against you. They are amongst the greatest of counter revolutionary elements today notwithstanding their sincere belief in servitude to Euro-Americans. The Integrationist accused Garvey of hating whites. He didn't hate whites, he simply loved his own people. On January 1st 1924 Garvey published a statement setting forth what his organization (Universal Negro Improvement Association, UNIA) believed in. The statement read in part,

> *"It [the UNIA] believes that the Negro race is as good as any other, and therefore should be as proud of itself as others are."*
>
> *It believes in the spiritual Fatherhood of God and the Brotherhood of Man."*
>
> *It believes in the social and political physical separation of all peoples to the extent that they promote their own ideals and civilization, with the privilege of trading and doing business with each other..."* [36]

An integrationist fails to realize the extent to which he is bound to his Euro-American master who at any time can allow him or not allow him to "hang out" as the common expression goes. The integrationist rightfully say from the point of view of their subjective experiences, *"the white man giveth and the white man taketh away"*. This is an apparent truth to the

[35] Philosophy and Opinions of Marcus Garvey, Centennial Edition 1887-1987, Vol.2 p. 294.
[36] ibid, Vol. 1 pp 81

integrationist since the Euro-Americans have given him employment and all else that he has and it is the Euro-Americans who have the power to take his employment and all else that he has away. Euro-Americans have allowed him to buy a house nearby and they can foreclose or otherwise seize this property at their will. Most integrationist refuse to accept the truth of their condition, namely that they have no liberty and are mere servants of Euro-Americans. The integrationist reinforces in the minds of his wife and children that as an individual he is of little worth. He is only a middle man. One whose only purpose is to receive and pass on to his family members the charity of his masters who would prefer not to *"dirty their hands"* with a more direct conveyance. The African-American integrationist, even the so called prosperous ones are nothing more than *"holders in due course"* of the embellishments of affluence. In other words he is the temporary custodian of wealth created by others. Whatsoever he has is a consequence not of his own creativity but the end result of his service to Euro-Americans. These gifts for good service on the part of the integrationist are not only paid for by virtue of him having performed *"good service"*, but paid for also in cash. Imagine being told by the American congress that you have just been awarded the civilian equivalent of the Congressional Medal of Honor, the Freedom Award. Imaging standing in front of the President of the United states who has the medal in his hand, ready to pin it on your breast. He says to you,

> *"Boy you've done a good job. We're going to give you this medal now. That'll be $9.95 please to cover medal manufacturing cost."*

This is what we face as a people and what the integrationist in particular faces. The integrationist is told in so may words,

> *"Boy you've done a fine job serving us within the lower rungs of corporate America. In return for your good service we're going to allow you the privilege of living next door to us. Now that'll be $300,000 for the mortgage please."*

145

Thousands and thousands of African Americans who became secure in their positions within corporate America found themselves first fired after having been last hired. Thousands more who mistakenly thought they had been hired as a result of merit, discovered that they were only filing "*set aside affirmative action*" slots. Any African American who in 1992 thinks his "expertise" is essential to Euro-America should be reminded that they have enough of their own experts. They don't need us. We must stop denying a fundamental fact which is that we are no longer needed in America. Cotton and tobacco are now processed by machines. Not only are we not needed, we have become wards of the state, sapping the resources of the general society by draining the state treasury. We produce nothing. We create nothing. We only take (whenever we can). This is an unpleasant fact, one that many, if not most, of us will deny, but a denial of truth does not make truth, untrue. Denial of truth merely reinforces falsehood and ignorance. We ought to stop the practice of denial. Marcus Garvey wrote,

> "...*We do not expect the white man to rob himself, and to deprive himself, for our racial benefit. How could you reasonably expect that, in an age like this, when men have divided themselves into racial and national groups, when the one group has its own interest to protect as against that of the other?*

> "*The laws of self-preservation force every human group to look after itself and protect its own interest; hence so long as the American white man or any other white man, for that matter, realizes his responsibility, he is bound to struggle to protect that which is his and his own, and I feel that the Negro today who had been led by the unscrupulous of our race has been grossly misguided, in the direction of expecting too much from the civilization of others.*" [37]

---

[37]   ibid Vol. 2 pp 103

An African American who loves liberty cannot be an integraionist. In the context of the American socio-policical situation, he notion of integration is a direct contradiction to the notion of liberty. You simply cannot love liberty and at the same time believe in integration. If you say you do, you demonstrate that you do not understand the meaning of liberty. Millions of African Americans have been duped into celebrating the memory of Dr. Martin Luther King without realizing that to celebrate Dr. King is to celebrate a loss of liberty. I'll take it a step further. To celebrate Dr. King is to celebrate slavery. Integration is nothing more than a sophisticated form of slavery. As a practical matter, whites reject integration. In the minds of most whites,

"the slaves have outlived their usefulness so why have them living next door draining resources rather than contributing to society".

No self respecting Euro-American believes that he cannot prosper unless an African American lives next door. Likewise no self respecting African American should believe that he can't prosper unless he is near Euro-Americans.

We must stop denying another simple truth. Euro-Americans are our adversaries and as such they are under no obligation to guard our unique interest. Their obligation is to guard their own interest and this they have been doing rather well. It is we who have not shouldered the responsibility of defining, cultivating and defending our interest. Those of us who think that Euro-Americans have any obligation to insure our prosperity are guilty of the "forty acres and a mule" syndrome. Those of you who think like this will continue to wait for presents not forthcoming. While you wait, you will continue to be penniless and hungry.

STUDY OUR SITUATION SCIENTIFICALLY

We can now begin to discuss in broad terms the specific task of our revolutionary efforts, the details of which we can discuss in our section on implementing the revolutionary alternatives.

It does not take a scholar to know that the basic purpose for the importation of Africans onto the American mainland was to have them work as slaves. It was never the intent of the "founding fathers" or the framers of the constitution that these slaves or their decedents be entitled to any other way of life than that of a slave. Affirmative action and set aside programs have always existed for us. We were set aside for the purpose of slavery and affirmatively put to that vocation. We were the wards of the state then, and are the wards of the state now. The masters had to care for us, feed us, think for us. Our general welfare was a direct result of the character of the Euro-American master. If the master was abusive, we were abused. If the master were not abusive we were not abused. If the master wanted to raise cotton, we picked cotton. If the master wanted to develop fertilizer, we would by necessity have to shovel cow manure. If the master wanted you to procreate you did. If the master did not want you to procreate, you didn't. The master never consulted you on matters of politics, domestic or international. You were not consulted on the national deficit or any thing that could increase your particular station in life. It was intended from the beginning that the master benefit from your labors not that you as a slave should benefit from his or even your own. Your sole function was supplementary to the master's primary purpose. It was not within the plan that you be anything other than a supplement to your master. Nothing is different today. Ask most Euro-Americans about establishing a separate black state and they'll laugh. It is inconceivable to the average Euro-American that an African American could be responsible enough to run his own personal affairs, let alone an entire nation. It is inconceivable because African American integrationist have not demonstrated that they have the desire to run their affairs. At all turns the integrationist sends the following message to white America,

"we don't believe we are competent as a race. We believe we must be near you in order to survive. We need you to tell us how to live and what to do. We beg you to let us

live beside you. We've marched on Washington to beg you for the privilege."

Such a view constitutes race hatred. The integrationist hates his own race. Rev. Alexander Crumwell wrote,

"Races like families, are the organisms and the ordinance of God; and a race feeling, like the family feeling is of divine origin. The extinction of race feeling is just as possible as the extinction of family feeling. Indeed a race is a family. The principle of continuity is as masterful in races as it is in families-as it is a nation" [38]

In the recesses of their private quarters, Euro-Americans laugh at the integrationist position. When they laugh they show the disdain and contempt such a position deserves. The integrationist position is diametrically opposed to the separatist position. Speak of integration and you will be laughed at. Speak of independence and separation and you will draw serious attention from many Euro-Americans who are deathly afraid of a truly liberated African American who would not be under their control.

Many Euro-Americans and many freed slaves of the 19th century associated the notion of emancipation of the slaves with totally separate and autonomous slaves in one form or another. One of the clearest rationals for a separation of freed slaves from the perspective of Euro-Americans was put forth by Charles F. Mercer of Virginia as he introduced a series of resolutions which passed the Virginia Assembly in 1826. They called on the government to settle Virginia's freed slaves in the North West part of America. It was important to white Americans that the freed blacks be kept as far away as possible from enslaved blacks. Mercer states,

"..many thousands of individuals in our native State...are restrained from manumitting their slaves...by the mel-

[38] Alexander Crumwell, The Race Problem in America: An Address, 1888, Africa and America: Addresses and Discourses (Springfield Mass, 1891, p.39-57)

ancholy conviction that they cannot yield to the sugges-tions of humanity without manifest injury to their coun-try. " [39]

Mercer believed that free blacks were a danger to the peace of the state and reduced the value of slave property elsewhere. There were other rationals for deporting freed slaves on a voluntary basis or upon compulsion. The basic rationals usually encompassed the desire for the American government to establish colonies in the Caribbean and the Latin Americas for commercial and military purposes. The American President, Abraham Lincoln, was a staunch advocate of slave expatriation and resettlement outside of the United States. Lincoln believed that the only long term solution to the race question in America was separa-tion of the races. He invited a delegation of African Americans to the White House on August 14 1862 to hear his ideas and plans for resettling the emancipated slaves in Central America.[40] In his first and second inaugural addresses Lincoln stated his desire for the departure of emancipated slaves.[41] The British and French governments were aware of Lincoln's feelings. Their own national interest were served by receiving emancipated American slaves as contract laborers in their respective colonies. On September 28 1862, the British charge d'affaires in Washington D.C., William Stuart held meetings with members of Lincoln's cabi-net and finally reported to his superiors that the American government was ready to enter in an ar-rangement,

[39]   Henry Noble Sherewood, The Formation of the American Colonization Society, Journal of Negro History, V2. No.3 (July 1917): pp 212-13
[40]   see "Address on Colonization to a Deputation of Negroes", The Collected Works of Abraham Lincoln, 1809-1865, ed. Roy Prentice, vol.5 1953-55
[41]   see A Compilation of the Messages and Papers of the Presidents, 1789-1897, ed. James D. Richardson, Vol 6:5, Abraham Lincoln, First Inaugural Address

"..for the purpose of enabling Her Majesty's government to transport from this country such of the negroes who have lately been, or who may become, emancipated, as many as may be willing to emigrate to Her Majesty's West Indian or to her tropical possessions" [42]

Because of potential commercial and military tensions between America and England as well as France, these negotiations broke down in the form they were taking. Lincoln's cabinet was split on the notion of expatriating emancipated slaves. The chief arguments against the idea centered around the concern that resettling slaves in British or French colonies would provide these countries with labor and expertise that may one day be turned around against American interest. [43] The British were aware of this sentiment and commented on it in the correspondence of Lord Lyons, British minister to the United States . Notwithstanding a divided cabinet, President Lincoln endorsed two other attempts to rid America of emancipated slaves. These were the Chiriqui program introduced in a cabinet meeting by Lincoln's Secretary of the Interior Caleb B. Smith on Sept. 26 1862 and the ill fated Ile A'Vache program, brain child of Bernard Kock that began in April 1863.

[42]   Letter, William Stuart to Earl Russell, Sept. 28, 1862, Public Record Office, London, C.O. 884/2

[43]   A general view with respect to the desirability of receiving emancipated American slaves was expressed by Lieutenant Governor Edward Eyre of Jamaica who in a letter to the British Colonial Office wrote that the American emancipated slaves were more desirable than immigrants from other places. Eyre expressed his view that the emancipated American slaves were "of industrious habits, and superior as a class than the present peasantry of the West Indian islands", See: Lieutenant. Governor Eyre to the Duke of Newcastle, July 5, 1862. Confidential Prints, West Indies: Correspondence Respecting the Emigration of Free Negroes from the United States to the West Indies, C.O. 884/2, Public Record Office, London

[44]   Letter, Lord Lyons to earl Russell, Dec. 26 1862, ibid

The Chiriqui program sought to resettle emancipated slaves to Central America but was abandoned because of the protest of Guatemala and San Salvador who thought the plan nothing more than an underhanded attempt on the part of the United States government to carry out its territorial expansion under the Manifest Destiny doctrine. The emancipated slaves were thought to be nothing more than U.S. agents entering into Central America for the purpose of taking over the respective Central American countries under the direction of the U.S. government and with it's total support. The Ile A'Vache program began with a group of freed slaves under the direction of Kock emigrating to the Haitian island of Ile A'Vache. This island had been leased by President Fabre Geffard of Haiti to Kock for a period of 20 years. The project failed for a number of reasons including disease, and local conflicts. Lincoln finally ordered a U.S. transport ship to A'Vache in February 1864 to bring back any of the group who had survived and were willing to return.[45]

There have been several attempts on the part of African Americans to secure their liberty by a repatriation to Africa. One of the earliest of these efforts was that of a prosperous African American named Paul Cuffee. Cuffee was a rich trader and whaling ship owner who lived in the state of Massachusetts during the early 1800's. After spending much of his time trying to gain political rights for of free African Americans in Massachusetts, he ultimately turned his attention to Africa and in particular the area known as Sierra Leone. In 1815, at his own expense Cuffee settled thirty-eight African Americans in Sierra Leone. Cuffee died September 7, 1817 without completing his mission of resettlement.[46]

The West African country of Liberia was settled by freed American slaves.[47] The work to settle this area of Africa was

[45]   see Abraham Lincoln to Edwin M. Stanton, Messages & Papers of the Presidents, 6:232-33.

[47]   Sheldon H. Harris, Paul Cufee, Black American, and the African Return, New York, 1972, pp. 38-39.

[48]   For a primary source of data on freed and recaptured slave immigrants to Liberia there is a rare U.S. Government document maintained

begun by the American Society for Colonizing the Free People of Color of the United States which became known as the American Colonization Society (founded in December 1816 by such notables as Robert Finley, Samuel J. Mills, Henry Clay, Francis Scott Key and Judge Bushrod Washington).[48] The purpose of the ACS was to provide a retreat for emancipated slaves either in Africa or the continental United States. It is worth while that we take an admittedly brief look at the history of Liberia, learn some lessons, and apply them to our own efforts.

With the encouragement of U.S. President James Monroe, the first freed American slaves settled in what is now Liberia in 1822. They secured land from indigenous tribal chiefs by bartering utensils, weapons and other items. The first settlement was governed by white men on behalf of the American Colonization Society but soon the area became an independent republic (1847). The history of Liberia up until the year 1980 was one in which the ex-American slaves formed a ruling elite and repressed the native peoples. This elite in time became multi-millionaires through their influence and at the Schomburg Center for Research in Black Culture, New York Public Library, New York. The document is titled US, Congress, Senate, US Navy Department, showing the number of Emigrants and recaptured Africans sent to the colony of Liberia by the government of the United States...together with a census of the colony and a report of its commerce. &c. September 1843: Senate Document No. 150, 28th Cong., 2d sess., 1845.

For additional information on how these immigrants fared in trade and commerce along the African west coast, see Yankee Traders, Old Coasters, and African Middlemen: A history of American Legitimate Trade with West Africa in the Nineteenth Century, G.E. Brooks (Brookline Mass 1970). For a wealth of references on all aspects of immigrant life in Liberia see Behold the Promised Land: A History of Afro-American Settler Society in Nineteenth-Century Liberia, Tom W. Schick (John Hopkins University Press 1977)

[48] For a complete history of this society, see Philip J. Staudenraus, The African Colonization Movement, 1816-1865 (New York 1961) and Penelope Campbell, Maryland in Africa: The Maryland State Coloniza- tion Society, 1831-1857 (Urbana 1971)

advantages gained by government office. The freed slaves had certainly achieved physical separation from the Americans but in many ways retained the attitudes and values of white America. All throughout the history of Liberia, the Americo-Liberian ruling elite attempted to duplicate as much of what they had seen in America as they could. Sanford J. Ungar writes about modern Liberia,

"Symbols of American influence abound in the capital. The country's red, white, and blue flag...looks as if it were designed by some Liberian relative of Betsy Ross. Monrovia's police wear hand-me-down summer uniforms from the New York Police Department. The Roxy Theater is next door to the Travolta Boutique, and bacon cheeseburgers are on nearly every menu. Videotapes of old episodes of 'Sanford and Son' are very much in demand...The Americo-Liberian regime built a remarkably faithful rendition of the U.S. Capitol, complete with House and Senate chambers and committee rooms in which a charade of the American system could be practiced..." [49]

The barbarous treatment slaves in America received was mirrored by the "Americo-Liberian" class towards the native peoples. The ruling elite of Americo-Liberians had been at the receiving end of a vicious system of deprivation, physical control, and slave labor back in America. They extended the native peoples no better treatment than that which they received from the Euro-Americans. The resettled slaves created a system of class elitism and exclusion with themselves being at the top of the pyramid. This continued for well over a century. The result was the development of two classes within Liberia, a very rich minority of African-American descent who ruthlessly oppressed the broad extremely poor majority. Liberty gained for the freed slaves turned into tyranny for the native population. This protracted history of elitism and

[49]   Sanford J. Ungar, Africa: The People and Politics of an Emerging Continent, 1986, Simon & Schuster Inc., p.101-102

indifference to those outside the ruling class was the seed of discontent and frustration on the part of the indigenous peoples. This resentment resulted in the overthrow of the ruling class headed by Liberian President William Tolbert, a grandson of freed slaves from South Carolina. The coupe took place in April of 1980 by Master Sergeant Samuel Doe of the Liberian army whose roots were native. Sergeant Doe's forces were known as the People's Redemption Council (PRC). The PRC began to slaughter the Americo-Liberian elite. Members of the Tolbert family who were ruling Liberia were killed. Adolphus B. Tolbert, the son of President W. Tolbert sought refuge in the French embassy in Monrovia. After a couple months Doe's forces stormed the embassy, seized and imprisoned him. He was shot a few months latter. Some Americo-Liberians were able to escape and take refuge in the United States outside Washington D.C. It is rather ironic that the migration of American freed slaves to Liberia can be described in Tolstoian style as follows,

> "In the early 1800 some freed American slaves wished liberty and a homeland of their own. They proclaimed a love of liberty and settled themselves in West Africa whereupon these lovers of liberty oppressed the native peoples. The freed slaves formed a government that legitimized their oppressive policies. The native peoples became angry and expelled the freed slaves who then returned to the land of their former masters."

Sergeant Doe inherited a system of government that had been riddled with corruption and leveraging for personal gain. After Doe's many trials and mistakes, he has managed to restore some normalcy to Liberia.

The freed slaves missed their opportunity to become the true light of Africa. Under a more enlightened leadership, we may have seen a nation of decedents of freed slaves with a well developed agricultural and industrial base and a standard of living rivaling that of the most advanced industrial nation. Instead it can effectively be argued that Liberia became the leader in Africa of corruption where even honored badges of

state, notably diplomatic passports and other State level
Cabinet positions were sold for profit to white foreigners who
wore these badges of office without any intent to serve the
nation and every intention of personal profit.

The lessons to be learned from the Liberian experience are many. Chief among them is the importance of
becoming not only physically separate but spiritually separate
from our enemies. We must understand the way in which our
enemy thinks but we must not think like our enemy. The
scriptures say that we should *"envy not the oppressor and
choose none of his ways"*. We do well to take this advice. Our
revolutionary efforts must not be undermined by our own lack
of insight and compassion for others. It must not be undermined by a corrupted spirit with an excessive attention to
profit at the expense of our fellow man. This is the very
character of our enemy which has finally encouraged us
towards revolutionary activity. So it was that the indigenous
Liberian peoples were motivated to revolt against the decedents of American slaves and so it will be wherever we are
should we, through a perverse spirit, motivate others to revolt
against us. The St. Thomas native, Edward Wilmot Blyden was
one of the more brilliant black spokesman for separation. He
drew a correlation between true liberty and separation from
Euro-Americans. Blyden was prophetic when he wrote,

> *"...our prosperity depends as much upon the wholesome
> and elevating influence we exert upon the native popu-
> lation, as upon the progress we make in agriculture,
> commerce and manufacturing."* [50]

He cautioned that a repression by freed slaves of the indigenous West African peoples of Liberia would result in catastrophe.

We cannot begin our revolution with the minds of
tyrants. Vigilance, and good social order do not imply nor
require tyranny. The one brings about freedom, the other is

[50]   Edward Blyden, The Call of Providence to the Descendants of Africa
in America, in Negro Social and Political Thought, 1850-1920: Represen-
tative Text, Howard Brotz (New York 1966), p.124

sure to result in chaos. We must do a better job than that done by the early settlers of Liberia. Our personal experiment with Liberty must not degenerate into an example of ineptness and tragedy.

At very best you can describe the relationship between ourselves and the general society as **Irrational Colonialism**. Typically a colonial power invades a foreign territory, subjugates it's inhabitants and takes control of the natural resources of that territory to include, if necessary, a seizure of the actual land for settlement of their own people as well as territorial expansion. The Europeans of the 19th century colonized Africa to exploit the natural resources of the continent. The inhabitants were put to work cultivating or processing these resources for the benefit of the colonizing power. The Europeans were forced to give up their colonies and withdraw to their own countries. Our situation in America is rather unique. We were the natural resource the colonizing power was interested in. The Americans rather than set up shop in Africa, took Africans out of Africa and made them "set up shop" in America. Now that we are not serving our original purpose, the colonial power, in our case the Americans, can not withdraw back to their own country. They are already in their own country by right of conquest. It is we that would have to withdraw back to our respective countries. The majority of us did not, at the time slaves were being repatriated to what is now Liberia, neither would the majority of us repatriate today without being forced to. The Europeans were the political and military enemies of the peoples they colonized. The Americans are our enemies. Only a fool denies this. We find ourselves in the unique position of a colonized people occupying the land of our enemy, rather than our enemy occupying our land. This is utterly backwards when viewed from a historical perspective. This is why I say that the colonialism of the Americans is an Irrational Colonialism when viewed from the perspective of the Americans. From our perspective as decedents of African slaves living in America, we have been *"get-in over"* as the colloquial expression goes.

We also find that we are so estranged from our natural homeland (Africa) that we have no desire to ever return

157

there. The unique character of American irrational colonialism as applied to us, combined with our desire for liberty provide us with our central contradiction and dilemma. It is this contradiction between our desire for liberty and the unique character of irrational colonialism that present the core of our problem and our fundamental challenge. This contradiction must be resolved if we are ever to prosper as a people. Let me summarize:

African Americans are the descendants of a defeated people.

Even though we are a defeated and colonized people, we are occupying the land of our enemies rather than our adversary occupying any land we own. This is irrational when viewed from the perspective of our adversary.

We do not intend to return to our original homeland (Africa). This is also irrational on our part but will not change.

We want to prosper. We are not prospering.

We must create a rational condition from an irrational condition. The central question now becomes "How?". It is a question that revolutionary leaders of the past have had to ask many times over.

DEVISE THE REVOLUTIONARY ALTERNATIVES: (WHAT IS TO BE DONE?)

We must devise a rational alternative to our present irrational condition. That is, we must devise a plan that will alter the colonial/colonized character of the relationship between ourselves and Euro-Americans. The plan must permit for our socio-economic and military independence from the Euro-Americans. The plan must provide not only 'for our continued occupation of the land upon which we currently reside but also that we own and control it absolutely. Such a plan presents some unique challenges but if we understand that all things man wishes to achieve he can, if he is willing to work diligently and make sacrifices. We can meet the challenges and prevail over our adversaries as long as we believe ourselves competent to do so. If we do not believe we can, we will fail to develop a viable prosperity plan. The status quo will remain. We will continue to be a disgrace in the eyes of our women and children and in the eyes of the world.

We must never forget or primary goal which is independence from the Euro-Americans. We must not forget the elements of this dependency. In other words we must not forget that we depend on them for our food, clothing, shelter, defense, and justice. Our goal of liberty must focus narrowly upon achieving independence in these areas. I say narrowly in the context of not allowing ourselves to become distracted by anything outside of the focus of our mission. Our goal of liberty is beset with many problems and many headaches. Some of the problems will seem insurmountable. But all of the problems that will arise will have a solution. It remains only for us to grasp what that solution is. There are some prerequisite conditions necessary before we begin to achieve our goal. The first prerequisite is our first mission.

MISSION STATEMENT #1: We must rid ourselves of the "30/60 minute problem/solution fault".

Our youth have been raised on an unhealthy diet of television images that portray fanciful and unrealistic pictures of life. Our youth have become impatient in large part because they see half hour to hour long television programs in which all the problems of the world are realized and totally resolved within that space of time. Day after day, year after year, our youth become infected with the 30/60 minute syndrome. When they resort to selling drugs to buy a luxury car, it is in large part due to their impatience. They want what they want, and they wan it now! They lack the ability to set long range goals and commit themselves to a steady course of action designed to achieve their goals. They are easily frustrated and try to take the easy and quick way to "success". The goal of liberty requires patience, hard work, sacrifice, and struggle. Our goal is such that upon commitment to it, you may never see it realized in your lifetime. It may be your children or grandchildren who reap the benefits of your labors. You must be prepared for this. Our goal will take more than 30 minutes or an hour to achieve. Those who are not able to rid themselves of the disease of impatience will drop out of the race shortly after beginning. These people will have shown themselves to be unworthy of liberty. Liberty requires hard work and sacrifice, usually of an extreme nature. The condition we find ourselves in has been developing for hundreds of years. It will take a long time to alter this condition. Our first revolutionary goal therefore is to rid ourselves of our character flaws, in particular the 30 minute/one hour problem/solution fault.

I said earlier we are the colonial subjects of an irrational colonialism. This irrational colonialism is irrational from a historical perspective as well as the contemporary perspective of the Euro-Americans. However from our perspective, this irrational colonialism gives advantages, opportunities and resources never before available to a colonized people. For as long as we are able, we must exploit the internal contradictions of irrational colonialism to our advantage. Chief of these contradictions is the fact that we occupy the land of the colonial power (the Euro-Americans). This is an utter reversal of the normal situation. Moreover, the colonial power, in their irrationality, strain the national treasury by creating programs designed to permit us to occupy even more of their land and even own the land. This is to our advantage and to the disadvantage of the Euro-Americans. Our goal of liberty will exploit this phenomena but not depend on it as though this irrational condition will exist forever.

As we move closer to consolidating our goals, we can expect that the Euro-Americans will attack our goal of liberty by at least mitigating the irrationality of their colonialism. The contradictions inherent in this colonialism will not always be there to exploit. So we must "strike while the iron is hot", consolidate our gains and be prepared to defend them should it prove a tactical necessity.

For the moment, the task of acquiring land is temporarily solved, that is most of us have a place to live. In the neighborhoods where we live, generally there are no Euro-Americans. We therefore are the majority people in our own neighborhoods. Another way of stating this is to say that along interior lines we are the majority but along exterior lines we are the minority. Along interior lines, we must cultivate total control. In time we will own the land and structures we now occupy. This will take much in the way of capital resources. Such capital resources or money is acquired through work and trade. We shall now begin ᵗ ⱼ draw a general outline of our revolutionary goals which will lead us to true liberty.

MISSIC N STATEMENT #2: We must cultivate commercial relationships with foreign nationals (preferably African nationals) interested in doing business with us in the areas of our needs.

The easiest of our goals of independence is that of independence in clothing. We must identify those among us who are able and willing to travel to Africa and purchase or manufacture cloth. This cloth will then be shipped back to us whereupon conversion of the cloth into functional garment wear can be done by African Americans. There are enough women with sewing machines who can be assembled to perform this task. The women will be paid for their labor and the finished products will be sold. The sale of the products can take place in individual homes or in small stores which we now occupy. It is important that we alter our purchasing habits. We can alter our purchasing habits when we redefine our notions of what constitutes "attractive". Right now, Euro-American fashions are seen as attractive and African fashions not attractive. We must alter this thinking. However, in the short term it is not essential that we alter our sense of the esthetic. If Euro-American fashions are what is desired, then it only becomes important that the stylist and pattern cutters here make finished garments in a style appropriate and attractive for the African American market. In other words we can cut cloth in the shape of existing fashions using existing color patterns or we can cut cloth in the shape of African dress using African color patterns, or we can do both. We can cut cloth using any pattern style and color style we choose. The important thing is that we are the ones buying and manufacturing the cloth and turning it into finished garment wear. African Americans are currently buying their clothing from Euro-American owned or Korean owned clothing stores. We must boycott them and buy from ourselves. What greater flattery to our nature can there be than to wear clothing for African Americans designed by African Americans. This is far better than to wear clothing for African Americans designed by the Euro-Americans.

There are already African American men who are planning to import cloth from Africa and turn it into sellable garment wear. All that remains is to support their efforts buy taking the same or less money you use now and buy the garments they manufacture or import. Should we begin to do this, clothing manufacturing plants can be built employing many both here and in Africa. One African American woman objected to this enterprise on the grounds that African cloth patters would be inappropriate in her work place. My response was three fold. First that the issue of inappropriateness is not an issue most African American women are concerned with. Most of them don't work in corporate America anyway. Second clothing styles and patterns can be constructed to suite the taste of women here in America. Finally she must understand that we are moving towards redefining the status quo of our material condition and of our mindset. The goal of our revolution is not to strengthen existing harmful thought patterns and practices. Our goal is independence in material condition and mental state. Such issues like appropriate dress should be defined by us and not for us. That woman's comments were counterrevolutionary. When you encounter this quality of comment you should not argue with the person. You should state the rational basis of your actions and thoughts explaining that they are revolutionary in character. You should be able, in some small way, to witness your belief in the goals of the revolution through some application of it in your daily life. Nothing is more persuasive than a person who is practicing what he preaches. When such a counterrevolutionary sees real benefits from the revolutionary goals as exemplified in your own life, he will me more inclined to participate in our revolutionary efforts. Talk is cheap. Action speaks louder than words. If I can demonstrate independence in thought and /or deed, I am more persuasive than if I can not. You are the ambassadors of the revolution at all times. All you need do is act consistent with the goals of the revolution. Do not allow yourself to become distracted by arguing with others.

In summary, because of the special and favorable conditions now existing in Africa, it is not inconceivable that African Americans could   form relationships with African nationals for the purpose of clothing manufacturing and sale. It is not inconceivable that African Americans would purchase these items. The clothing items can be of any pattern, plain or ornate, and be of any style. The important thing is that African Americans are engaged in an enterprise which relieves them from dependency upon Euro-Americans   for clothing. Independence is therefore advanced.

The issue of food production and distribution is vital. Food is life. Without it you die. It is in this area that the revolution demonstrates a critical weak spot. Food production implies land ownership and   highly specialized skills. We do not own land. We only occupy land. The land we occupy in general is land in the cities. Farming does not take place in cities. Remember our mission is to break the cycle of dependency upon Euro-Americans. It is this underlying principle of liberty we think about as we consider the question of food production and distribution.

Currently most African Americans buy their food from Euro-American owned supermarket chains. The food in these chains comes from food distribution centers. Food distribution centers receive food from several sources, store it and allocate it to the various food retail houses that you call supermarkets. Our task is to duplicate the efforts of the food distribution centers. At the very least this requires massive storage space either in central locations or in a multitude of interlinked smaller locations. There lies our first problem, that of space for food storage. The second problem is the identification of food sources. Food can be grouped general as perishable and not perishable. Perishable foods are fruits vegetables, meats and dairy products that are not in cans. Non perishable are dry goods and canned goods. The essence of independence is to manufacture both perishable and non-perishable foods. This requires land for cultivating crops, land for animal husbandry, and factories for food processing in the case of perishable and non-perishable foods. All of this is not within the means of the individual revolutionary efforts. It could be within the means of specialized revolutionaries who have acquired sufficient capital for land acquisition by engaging in such enterprises as "Liberty Clothing" ventures. "Liberty Clothing" is only one of many ventures that could be used to support "Liberty Farms". The manufacture of children's toys and artifacts for the home are well within the means of those who would take an interest in Liberty Clothing. Capital gained from these enterprises would support activities designed to extricate us from dependency on Euro-Americans for our food. A combined capital resource, that is, capital from the "Liberty" commercial ventures, together with capital investment from those few African Americans of wealth can facilitate both the Liberty ventures and the Liberty Farms.

MISSION STATEMENT #3: Identify African American businessmen and men of wealth who are willing to invest in Liberty Ventures.

A Who's Who in African American businessmen is available. These men must be contacted and given the opportunity to partake in our quest for Liberty. They must be impressed with possibilities of continuing to do business without having to rely upon Euro-Americans as their cliental. African Americans who have established a track record, ever so minor, of doing business with foreign nationals must serve as a model to these businessmen in order to impress them with the feasibility of joining our revolutionary efforts. We are not seeking mere philanthropy even from our own. We must demonstrate a facility with sound business practice in order to encourage the support of successful African American businessmen. It is the job of eloquent orators and men of vision, propagandist to be exact, to encourage successful African American businessmen to support the revolutionary goal of true Liberty.

MISSION STATEMENT #4: Let us be the authors of our own justice.

We must identify those of us who are gifted with an

even temperament and sound judgment. They must be men who are impartial and wise, senior in years and who have demonstrated the ability to endure hardship. These men must become judges. We ought not to take our disputes to the Euro-American courts. The quality of justice we receive from our adversaries is "no justice". An objective analysis of the legal system clearly demonstrates this. Furthermore there is no rational basis for believing that we shall ever receive true justice from the Euro-Americans in the future. Our quarrels and breeches of our law must be taken before our own wise men for decisions. Their decisions should be seen as binding and enforceable in the same way we were wiling to submit to the decisions and enforcement of the Euro-Americans through their court systems.

Our young men should be used as a police force under the direct supervision of senior members of our society. It should be preferred that this supervision be conducted by those among us who have had prior military training. They would be paid a salary since this would be their sole occupation for a time. Their salary would come from contributions made by the local community in combination with money they make as a group engaged in several Liberty ventures. Looking into the future, their salary would come from a system of tax assessments we determine just and appropriate. It is within these corps of police that our young men will learn discipline, organization and common effort. It is here that they will be imputed with a spirit of helping their fellow man rather than their present commitment to their own selfish and destructive aims alone. This police force is the seed of a future defense force. It is from this initial corps of men that our future military officer corps will be founded. Initially this corps of young policemen must be put to the task of true community service. In marked distinction to the police forces under the control of the Euro-Americans that do not act in our best interest, our young men will become the friends and protectors of the people and a front line guardian of their liberty. They will engage in such activities as helping senior citizens travel about, cleaning recreational parks and children's playground areas and guarding these parks and playgrounds against abusive use.

They will help residents clean streets and repair sidewalks and roads. They will be a hard working force put to utilitarian task as well as general police work. Their general police work will include identifying the two types of internal enemies we are certain to discover among us. Elsewhere in this book, I discuss at length these enemies.

Abandoned buildings in neighborhoods could be cleaned and used as temporary housing for persons who are to be brought before our judges. Other abandoned properties could be cleaned and refurbished by this corps of youth. Capital for rehabilitation would come from the various Liberty ventures. Judges in each area could assign on a priority/needs basis, these properties to families who would purchase them upon favorable terms.

IMPLEMENT THE REVOLUTIONARY OBJECTIVES

The implementation of our Revolutionary objectives was touched upon in the previous section. A detailed public discussion would be a violation of the security of our efforts in that it would take away any competitive advantages we develop. It shall suffice for now to re-state our general objectives which are to form relationships with African-Americans who have, or are about to conduct business enterprises in Africa. We must find ways to engage in symbiotic relations with such persons so that there will develop a mutual prosperity. We must also be willing to engage in such ventures directly. Local "Block Captains" should meet regularly to discuss and implement service type industries in their immediate area. The central theme must be "Which services are we contracting Euro-Americans to perform? Who among us can perform the same service?" Where there is no answer to the latter question, those present should commit their sons or daughters to cultivating the skills necessary to provide the services. Skilled craftsman in our areas should be encouraged to spend one or two hours a week instructing the youth of the particulars of their skill. In time these "apprentices" will master their trade and be able to perform the functions which now only Euro-

Americans are performing in our neighborhoods. We must incorporate the slogan "Replace Euro-American workmen with African American workmen" into our thinking or to re-state it using our very own unique and expressive dialect, "White was right, but Black is back. There's a new thing happening now."

DEFEND THE REVOLUTIONARY ACHIEVEMENTS

If throughout revolutionary efforts, we achieve true liberty, that is, we are no longer dependent upon the Euro-Americans for our food, clothing, shelter and the justice we receive, it would be folly not to defend our accomplishments.

The achievements we make will forever be refined and further developed. Obviously all that we build can be undermined if we are not vigilant. No nation of people can afford complacency. We are no exception to this rule. The task of defending revolutionary goals is a most grave. It must be approached with profound seriousness as well as an unbending intent of purpose. Defense of our achievements must not be approached with pre-conceived and fixed ideas that are too specific and limiting. To do so would be to adopt a specific action policy without first having studied what our situation requires. During the course of achieving our revolutionary goals we will have experienced many setbacks, many "ups and downs". We will have seen conditions change from day to day presenting us with a multitude of challenges. This constant change of conditions can be called the "dynamic conditions" of our revolution. So it is with the matter of our defense. We can not afford fixed notions or notions derived without a scientific study of our unique situation because the challenges that we will face will be dynamic, that is the nature of the challenges will change constantly. We must be fluid in our thinking and practices. We must be able to meet each adverse condition with the proper remedial response. This requires a supreme mental strength. It requires that we cultivate a force amongst us that is devoid of opinion and judgment. It must be a force of young men capable of the most tender affection and compassion yet also capable of extreme devastation and cruelty. This force will

167

be our own Objective Defense Force. More precisely, it will be the **New Reconstruction Objective Defense Force.** If compassion is called for, then without thought, without hesitation our **NRODF** (New Reconstruction Objective Defense Force) will be capable of unequaled compassion. If destruction is called for, then without thought, without hesitation, without concern for personal safety, our **NRODF** will act in ways that will surely instill fear in the hearts of our enemies. At all times our **NRODF** will act in compliment to the challenges we face. They will meet all challenges to our revolutionary effort with rational remedial action designed to preclude further counter revolutionary acts.

The young men who will compose our defense force will have undergone an extremely rigorous intellectual, physical, and spiritual training. Many of those who begin the training will not be able to complete it. Only the most fit to serve will "graduate" form the intensive training. These young men will be the flower of our nation, the guardians of our peace. Those who fail to complete this training will be allowed to serve in a secondary defense force or neighborhood guard. It is important that all of our young men undergo some type of structured discipline. They must be taught to think as a unit, to respond as a unit, and to become resolutely committed to our nation as a whole. This is in marked contrast to their present attitudes and nature which encourages selfishness, disrespect for their own kind in general, and for African-American authority in particular. Our adversary has encouraged contemporary African American youth towards their present attitudes as part of their design to subvert our evolution to the condition of true independence. However, almost all of the blame for the self-destruct nature of our youth can be placed on our own shoulders. Every man and woman is the "front line" guardian and role model for their own child. Where parents raise their children in permissive environments, you can expect those children to develop into the irresponsible murderous monsters that many of them are today.

As I mentioned earlier, the primary mission of our **NRODF** is to defend the achievements of the revolution. Their specific mission will be to neutralize all external and internal enemies who seek to undermine or reverse our revolutionary achievements and throw us back into a state of dependency on the Euro-Americans. The task of the **NRODF** is to be a buffer between the social and industrial leaders and functions. The task of social and industrial development must continue with little if any interruption. The **NRODF** can go a long way to insure this. Let each of us commit our sons from the ages of 15 upwards to **NRODF** training. Let all men with military experience come forth to lend their assistance. Mothers release your sons. Expect them to perform with excellence. Do not cringe at the harshness of their conditioning. It is from the iron and fire of **NRODF** training camps that outstanding, upstanding, righteous young men will evolve ready to defend you. They will be intensely proud that they "had what it took" to complete training. Do not tolerate anything less than their best effort. Let all sons know that their mother's would rather see them dead than defeated. Revive the old Spartan slogan,

**"Come back Victorious,
carrying your shield, or dead on it !"**

CHAPTER-NINE

Final Advice and Summary

We have engaged in a fairly exhaustive discussion of the ugly nature of the American Black woman. I'll refer to her as the **Old World woman**. Your replacement for the Old World woman is your partner in **The New-Reconstruction**. We have discussed the factor of your *'Contributory Negligence'*. We have discussed the relationship between you and white America. We then came to a discussion of alternatives to wives in the form of women from other countries. Let's assume that you and a lady from another country have struck a harmonious personal note and that the two of you are now married. What is this experience going to be like for you? Let me back up a bit first. The more important thing to go over again is how are you going to conduct *yourself* with your new wife. Remember part of the New-Reconstruction involves the process of 'reconstructing' ourselves. We want to be sure we don't repeat the mistakes of the past which caused us to have to endure the **Old World woman**, that is to say, the American Black woman.

You know, there's no precedent for a rotten apple doing a flip and becoming fresh again. What is rotten is rotten. The Old World woman is rotten. She's not rehabilitative, at least not by you. Her brain washing has been too thorough. The level of her hostility towards you is too high. You, however, are. You are less brainwashed than she is and you're not hostile to yourself. *You* can rehabilitate you. The Old world woman changed from in character from being a co-operative, feminine, person to a hostile, person with masculine tendencies, that is masculine mannerisms and attitudes. [51] You, on the other

---

[51]   I have a couple friends who are currently doing a study on testosterone levels in women. Testosterone is the male hormone. It is their thesis that excess testosterone levels in women result in masculine traits. It is their position that the aggressiveness of woman's liberation types can be never

changed. You've been consistently passive for centuries and are still basically the same. In a strange way this consistent passivity has had a certain redeeming value. You've not become as *corrupted* in your thinking as the American Black woman. In a strange way, the fact that the white man has excluded you from participation in society has been a blessing in disguise. It has precluded you from being as duped as you might otherwise have been had you become a total participant in perverted white society. You have been affected, if only because of what amounts to an osmotic process. If you're around a pervert long enough, at least some of his perversion is going to rub off on you. But this osmosis has not been as deadly as the mental processes Black women have gone through, namely a conscience and open hostility to Black men and the brainwashing they have received while being in alliance with white society against you. You've both been brainwashed but Black women appear to have been brainwashed beyond redemption. It is vital that you become the new

counted for, at least in part, by an excess of testosterone in their system. These gentlemen avoid women who show signs of high testosterone levels. When I asked them how they determine a woman has a high testosterone level, one of them told me that the signs are, 1. small breast, 2. small buttocks, 3. thin thighs, 4. excess facial or leg hair, 5. tendency towards high stress jobs or jobs requiring aggressive personalities, 6. feeling compelled to prove the quality between men and woman. They concede that not every women who manifest these traits necessarily has high testosterone levels, but that they are possible signs of it. One of the gentlemen will be publishing the results of his research soon. For those of you who are inclined to research the scientific literature on this subject, someone suggested to me that you can try starting with the following papers, Testosterone Induced Mounting Behavior in Adult Female Rats Born In Litters Of Different Female To Male Ratios, Slob AK, et.al., PHYSIO BEHAV, 1982 Jun;28(6);1007-10, see also Relationship Between Seasonal Changes In Aggression, Plasma Testosterone and Photoperiod In Male Rhesus Monkeys, Michael RP et.al., PSYCHONEU-ROENDOCRINOLOGY 1981;6(2):145-58, also Cohabitation With A Female Activates Testosterone-Dependent Social Aggression In Male Rats Independently Of Changes In Serum Testosterone Concentration, Albert DJ et.al. PHYSIOL BEHAV 1988;44(6);735-40. These papers will lead you to others on the subject.

man of the **New-Reconstruction**. It is vital that all of your old thinking patterns and your old habits be utterly cast away. Your old patterns got you the ugly natured American Black women. Old patterns and old ideas applied to your **New-Reconstruction** wife will get you a **New-Reconstruction** wife who will in short time turn against you too. It's a simple matter of cause and effect. Do the things that will cause a catastrophe and the effect will be that a catastrophe will occur. We have to be certain we understand our past mistakes. A political theorist once wrote,

"...It is from failure that one derives lessons and corrects one's ideas so as to make them correspond to the laws of the external world. This is how one turns failure into success. This is exactly what is meant by failure being the mother of success, and by 'a fall into the pit, a gain in your wit'..." [52]

What were the catastrophic mistakes when you served as an **Old World Black Man** that had such a devastating effect upon the **Old World Woman**, that is to say, the American Black woman? They were as follows;

Obvious Failures
Failure to have a good Provider plan, that is failure to insure that you do not need the white man for food clothing and shelter.
Failure to have a good Protection plan. Failure to defend your women and children from white American aggression.

Subtle Failures
Excessive attention to pleasure, i.e. sports, gambling, drinking.
Integrationist ideology, or restated, the beggars mentality.
Lack of social creativity, i.e. failure to devise a social value system unique to, and for, your welfare as opposed to adopting the white system of values.
Failure to exercise general command quality leadership in

---
[52] On Practice, Mao Tse Tung

the household.

You must do something about all these failures. Never fail in these ways again with your **New-Reconstruction** bride. You must be able to take care of your family financially. You must have a value system that is humanitarian and exemplifies justice, as opposed to one which is purely capitalistic, individualistic and based on greed. You must not allow your family to be subject to abuse in any form from anyone, particularly your American enemies. You must cease to be an integrationist begging the general society for an extra crumb off their table. You must have enough self esteem to preclude you from such a demeaning practice. You must be the commander in chief of your household. You must abandoned such perverted and disgusting ideas as the equality of men and women and the resultant notion of shared power within a relationship. There is no shard power. *YOU* are power. From your *power*, all other persons in the household derive their *authority*. Your wife is given authority to implement the policies you design. You have the power to design the family's goals and overall tone. Your wife is given the *authority* to see that your policies are implemented. You had better see yourself as this ultimate power because believe you me, your **New-Reconstruction** woman *will* see you this way. Her cultural upbringing has conditioned her to see you as the King of the Castle in no uncertain terms. To the extent that you are not the ultimate power and authority in your household, you generate confusion in her mind and finally, contempt of your person. This is what happened to you with your Old World woman.

You have to keep tabs on yourself at all times in order to shake loose the vestiges of Old World corrupted thinking and habits. When my wife first arrived here, I remember setting off to go to the movies. I instinctively asked her which movie she wanted to see. The question shocked her! To her it was bizarre. I was supposed to determine which movie we were to see. This was my prerogative and mine alone. It was my duty. I would dictate, and she would follow. Anything else to her was bizarre and unacceptable. You see, a little thing like the decision process involved in going to the movies can contain the elements of corrupted thinking within us all. *You have to get rid of all of it.* I had gotten rid of most of it by the time my wife arrived but I still had enough perverse thinking left to cause problems. Work on yourself. Believe in your ability to make sound decisions based upon the evidence you've analyzed. Then act! Your **New-Reconstruction** wife will expect this of you. She wants to feel secure '*under your umbrella*'. Your Old World woman never felt secure. You were too wishy-washy, too weak, not resolute, afraid of command. Correct these faults. Though strength and moral courage are requisite for command, gentleness and compassion are also important qualities. Be gentle and compassionate with your new bride. Remember, your new wife is in a strange land with strange and perverted peoples, strange and perverted customs. It's a violent land full of hate and corruption. It's a land where men marry men. [53] She'll feel frightened and confused. She'll need you desperately during those first few years of her adjustment to this country. Don't introduce her to your Old World girlfriends with their hostile degenerate ways. This will only bring discord into your home. Your new wife will find the mannerisms and ideas of your Old World women repulsive. Your **New-Reconstruction** bride will hear the Old World woman speak with her disrespectful tongue, and see her behave in masculine ways. By exposing your new woman to this, she'll feel you've placed her in an uncomfortable position. It's like someone picking up a wad of shit and shoving it in your face with a smile while all the time showing no shame for the outrage. Wouldn't that make you feel uncomfortable? Don't expose her to the Old World woman if you can avoid it. It's only common sense. If you bring shit into your house, the air is going to stink. You bring these Old World women into your house, the air is going to stink. Out of pure envy and jealousy, the Old World woman will try her best to make sure your house stinks.

If your new woman seeks employment, you'll have to spend some time with her helping her overcome the confusion

[53]   The city of San Francisco recognizes a common law declaration of marriage between two homosexual men. Seattle Washington and Washington, D.C. have similar laws.

she is bound to have when she observes the women around her on the job. She'll come home and say things like *"I just don't understand these American girls, they're so....etc"* Let her know that you are very much aware of their repulsive conduct and attitudes and it is for this reason that you have rejected them. Your new lady will begin to appreciate the fact that you have a fundamental value system which precludes the repulsive conduct she witnesses in American women and Black American women in particular. My wife has noticed the differences in behavior between American women as a function of race. She differentiates how American white women act as compared to American Black women. She has discovered their common traits as well as their race specific traits. She finds them both puzzling but finds Black women more of a puzzle. In defense of Black women, I often try to explain to my wife the historical context which has made them the way they are. Yet still as a practical matter, there are less than a handful of American Black women who have an open invitation to our home. The air in my house is sweet with the aroma of harmony, joy and co-operation. I intend to keep it that way.

I've discused with many **Stage-4** Black men their concerns that the new women, once exposed to the American society will become like the Americans. I addressed this earlier but I'll say finally that anything in life can happen. It's all a matter of probabilities. If you're doing a proper job of being a New-Reconstruction man, you're not likely to have such a problem. Of course if you choose women from *"danger zone cultures"* as may exist in places in the Caribbean, you increase the odds that your woman will become like the American. You've got to remember that the ball is in your court. The overall tone of the household is your responsibility. You are the guide. You are the standard to which the rest of the family must measure itself. Any behavior which seek to stray from this standard must not be ignored, but put in check. All people in the world make errors. Your partner in the New-Reconstruction will make errors. It's up to you to insure that they cause no great damage. You'll find that your new woman is much more willing to adjust her behavior if she is made aware that something displeases you. Take charge. Be gentle, but assertive. Never forget you're in command. All eyes look to you. It is this attitude that your new woman will expect you to have, otherwise she too will loose respect for you. Many of you will have read this book and in your anger seen it as solely an **"attack on Black women"** or an **"attack on Black men"**. To those, I say, you failed to see the "total picture", the greater design of the book and its message. Accordingly, let me now acquaint you with it. The book uses a discussion of Black male-female relationships as a basis to call for two Black transformations or restated, two Black Revolutions within America. The **First Revolution** is a **Personal** one. It's internal. It deals strictly with the individual against himself. In particular, it's Black men undergoing a total re-shaping of their character. The book calls for Black men to evolve from being the passive, defensive, and easily distracted persons they currently are, to active, aggressive, ruthless, men resolved to correctly analyze their condition within America and then proceed to the **Second Revolution.** This personal revolution is a prerequisite for any subsequent stage. The personal revolution is demanding. It calls for the highest levels of honesty, integrity, and *courage.* It takes courage to face oneself in the mirror and come to grips with truths they may not want to see. It's easy to find fault in another but its hard to admit ones own faults. It's easier to face your external enemy in hand to hand combat than to engage in a fight to the death with 'self'. In such a fight, part of you dies. Either the noble side of you slays your degenerate side, or your degenerate side prevails against your noble side. In either case the individual will suffer the pains of a death of sorts. I call upon Black men to slay the degenerate side of their nature. I call upon you to gain victory over yourself.

In the book I call upon Black men to develop not just a Defensive survival plan, that is, a set of *"spare of the moment"*, incidental behaviors designed just to *"get by"* in life, but an aggressive, offensive strategy with tactics designed to stifle white aggression, in all its forms, against the participants of the **New-Reconstruction.** I defined earlier what the **New-Reconstruction** was. Let me quote Lt. Colonel R. B. Thieme Jr. (Ret),

"[The] Offensive is the only action by which a decision is gained! The only effective way to wage a war is to act on the offensive. Offensive action brings victory, while defensive action can only avoid or delay defeat...the defensive should be adopted only under these conditions: to assist offensive action elsewhere; to gain time; to compensate for weakness in other areas or to envelop the enemy." [54]

The *"spare of the moment"* approach to life is part of Old World thinking. It's a mere defensive approach to our "struggle" and must be abandoned as our primary strategy during the battles which take place in the First and Second Revolutions.

The **Second Revolution** is **Political** in nature. Its object is *partly* internal and partly external. The internal aspect of the Second Revolution refers not to the individual but to the group as a whole, that is the group of all those who are participants in the **New-Reconstruction.** It has two components. One component is socio-economic and spiritual development. The other component is an applied physical defense of the socio-economic and spiritual structures created under the first component. By this I mean an actual police or military structure designed by Black men. The purpose of said structures is to defend the participants of the **New-Reconstruction** against any *physical* assault our enemies may begin upon our people directly, or the socio-economic and spiritual structures created in the first component. Such an assault will come from an external enemy and/or from an internal enemy. The internal enemy will be of two types. There will be those who have made an open declaration of war against the **New-Reconstruction** and will be acting covertly within **New-Reconstruction** areas for the purpose of sabotage. I'll call these **Class-A** internal enemies. **Class-B** internal enemies are those who have made their way into the **New-Reconstruction** areas without having successfully undergone the **First Revolution**. Such a person or persons would still have vestiges of Old World thinking and habits. These persons are enemies without overt

[54] The Christian Warrior, R.B Thienne Jr. pp 25-26

intention, but they are enemies just the same. Their effect upon the **New-Reconstruction** would be adverse. They would undermine the progress of the **New-Reconstruction** by their Old World thinking and habits. As man thinks, so does he act. Old World thinking is the seed of Old World behavior. Old World behavior is what we have been identifying all throughout this book as having had a devastating effect on Blacks in America, particularly on American Black women. However **Class-B** enemies are less of a threat than **Class-A** only because they will be easy to detect. There would be an obvious distinction between **Class B** enemies and members of the **New-Reconstruction.** These Old Order Class-B enemies would think and act in ways totally at variance with New-Reconstruction Philosophy and Practice. They are easily identifiable. It is the **Class-A** types we must take extra care to guard against. They will try to sound like us and act like us yet all the while they'll be spreading dissention and engaging in sabotage against our efforts. The respective fate of either enemy historically has been banishment in the case of **Class-B** enemies, and judgement with *"extreme prejudice"* in the case of **Class-A** enemies.

Again, I use a discussion of Black male-female relationships as a vehicle towards understanding the need for such a revolution. I tried to demonstrate how Black men and women have been victims of a hostile attack upon our persons by white America. I suggest that whites have inflicted severe battle casualties upon us which have become manifest as passive and distracted Black men, and un-rehabilitative Black women. I suggested that the wounds inflicted upon the Black woman have been terminal. I suggested that Black women who have suffered wounds *have not* recovered and *will not* recover. I tried to motivate Black men to wake up and take political revolutionary action in the form of a regrouping and consolidation of what forces that are left, together with a recruitment drive for fresh troops. By "forces that are left", I meant **US**, that is to say, Black men, who I describe in the book as constituting the officer class of the **New-Reconstruction**. The *"fresh troops"* we recruit will be women from other countries who have not been tainted by a protracted experience in America with a pre

New Reconstruction, Old World, Black men.

The **First Revolution** gives rise to a new spirit within the Black man. This spirit is a ruthless obsession for facts and analysis without regard to the distractions pleasure brings. In other words, as an example of what I'm saying, basketball will no longer distract our thoughts and absorb our energies. The **Second Revolution** re-establishes our families. It creates a nation for all practical purposes separate and apart from the general population. This **Second Revolution** seeks political victory over our enemies through a fanatical determination to keep our *new families* in tack and impervious to outside influence. Such a protective hedge requires the development of a separate Black socio-economic structure from which we will operate.

I am under no illusion that the majority of Black men and women in America will transform their nature and become part of the **New Reconstruction** but as many as will join are welcome. If I have offended many of you, I felt it necessary in order that I may shock you into a state of reflection and analysis. Accordingly, I make no apology for my offensive pen.

Gentlemen, victory is sweet. To destroy ones enemies is divine. It's a phenomena more beautiful that anything you can imagine. Gentlemen. Victory is ours for the taking. **Let's take it!** .

"...for we are made a spectacle unto the world, and to angels, and to men..." 1 Cor 4:9

Peace, YOSHUA BARAK

180

APPENDIX A

No. 11. Total Population, by Race: 1960 to 1989

[As of July 1. Includes Armed Forces overseas. For derivation of estimates, see text, section 1]

YEAR	Total (1,000)	White (1,000)	Black (1,000)	Other races (1,000)	PERCENT— White	Black	Other races
1960	180.671	160.023	19.006	1.642	88.6	10.5	0.9
1970	205.052	179.644	22.801	2.607	87.6	11.1	1.3
1975	215.973	187.629	24.778	3.567	86.9	11.5	1.7
1980	227.757	195.571	26.903	5.283	85.9	11.8	2.3
1965	239.279	203.159	28.994	7.125	84.9	12.1	3.0
1989	248.762	209.326	30.788	8.647	84.1	12.4	3.5

No. 17. Projected Components of Population Change, by Race: 1995 to 2025

[Includes Armed Forces overseas. Projections are for middle series (series 14) for assumptions, see headnote, table 16. For explanation of methodology, see text, section 1]

YEAR AND RACE	TOTAL (Jan 1-Dec 31) Population at start of period (1,000)	Net increase [1] Total (1,000)	Per cent [2]	Natural increase Births (1,000)	Deaths (1,000)	Net civilian immigration (1,000)	RATE PER 1,000 MIDYEAR POPULATION Net growth rate	Natural increase Total	Birth rate	Death rate	Net civilian immigration rate
ALL RACES											
1995	259.238	1.767	0.68	3.517	2.275	525	6.8	4.8	13.5	8.7	2.0
2000	267.498	1.522	0.57	3.389	2.367	500	5.7	3.8	12.6	8.8	1.9
2005	274.884	1.433	0.62	3.399	2.465	500	5.2	3.4	12.3	8.9	1.8
2010	281.894	1.351	0.48	3.485	2.634	500	4.8	3.0	12.3	9.3	1.8
2025	297.926	622	0.21	3.357	3.235	500	2.1	0.4	11.3	10.9	1.7
WHITE											
1995	216.267	1.074	0.50	2.744	1.986	296	5.0	3.6	12.7	9.1	1.4
2000	221.087	837	0.38	2.602	2.038	273	3.8	2.5	11.7	9.2	1.2
2005	225.048	746	0.33	2.583	2.110	273	3.3	2.1	11.5	9.4	1.2
2010	228.637	674	0.29	2.839	2.238	273	2.9	1.8	11.5	9.8	1.2
2025	235.317	79	0.03	2.490	2.684	273	0.3	-0.8	10.6	11.4	1.2
BLACK											
1995	33.000	396	1.20	601	262	56	11.9	10.2	18.1	7.9	1.7
2000	34.939	379	1.08	597	272	54	10.8	9.2	17.0	7.7	1.5
2005	36.816	372	1.01	604	286	54	10.1	8.6	16.3	7.7	1.5
2010	38.653	358	0.93	616	312	54	9.2	7.8	15.9	8.0	1.4
2025	43.348	247	0.57	602	410	54	5.7	4.5	13.9	9.5	1.3
OTHER RACES											
1995	9.971	298	2.98	172	48	174	29.4	12.2	17.0	4.7	17.2
2000	11.472	305	2.66	190	58	173	26.3	11.4	16.4	5.0	14.9
2005	13.020	315	2.42	211	69	173	23.9	10.8	16.0	5.2	13.1
2010	14.604	319	2.18	230	84	173	21.6	9.9	15.6	5.7	11.7
2025	19.261	296	1.54	265	142	173	15.5	6.4	13.9	7.4	9.0

[1] Includes overseas admissions into, less discharges from, Armed Forces, not shown separately   [2] Percent of population at beginning of period.

Source: U.S. Bureau of the Census. Current Population Reports, series P-25, No. 1018.

181

Population

No. 14. Estimated Components of Population Change, by Race: 1960 to 1989

YEAR OR PERIOD	TOTAL (Jan. 1-Dec. 31)						RATE PER 1.000 MID-PERIOD POPULATION				
	Popula-tion at start of period (1,000)	Net increase [1]		Natural increase		Net civilian immigra-tion (1,000)	Net growth rate [1]	Natural increase			Net civilian immigra-tion rate
		Total (1,000)	Per-cent [2]	Births [3] (1,000)	Deaths (1,000)			Total	Birth rate [3]	Death rate	
ALL RACES											
1960	179,386	2,901	1 62	4,307	1,708	328	16 1	14 4	23 8	9 5	1 8
1965	193,223	2,315	1 20	3,801	1,830	373	11 9	10 1	19 6	9 4	1 9
1970	203,849	2,617	1 28	3,739	1,927	438	12 8	8 8	18 2	9 4	2 1
1975	214,931	2,165	1 01	3,144	1,894	449	10 0	5 8	14 6	8 8	2 1
1980	226,451	2,582	1 14	3,612	1,990	845	11 3	7 1	15 9	8 7	3 7
1985	238,207	2,325	0 98	3,761	2,087	650	9 7	7 0	15 7	8 7	2 7
1987	242,841	2,367	0 97	3,809	2,124	683	9 7	6 9	15 6	8 7	2 8
1988	245,208	2,409	0 98	3,913	2,171	667	9 8	7 1	15 9	8 8	2 7
1989	247,617	2,505	1 01	3,977	2,155	682	10 1	7 3	16 0	8 7	2 7
Annual averages:											
1960-1964	179,386	2,767	1 54	4,210	1,756	346	14 8	13 2	22 6	9 4	1 9
1965-1969	193,223	2,125	1 10	3,633	1,889	418	10 7	8 8	18 3	9 5	2 1
1970-1974	203,849	2,216	1 09	3,370	1,946	359	10 6	6 8	16 1	9 3	1 7
1975-1979	214,931	2,304	1 07	3,293	1,909	449	10 5	6 3	14 9	8 7	2 0
1980-1984	226,451	2,351	1 04	3,646	2,001	682	10 1	7 1	15 7	8 6	2 9
1985-1989	238,207	2,383	1 00	3,843	2,128	668	9 8	7 0	15 8	8 7	2 7
WHITE											
1970	178,692	2,050	1 15	3,095	1,687	327	11 4	7 8	17 2	9 4	1 8
1975	186,955	1,459	0 78	2,552	1,661	173	7 8	4 7	13 6	8 9	0 9
1980	195,143	1,272	0 65	2,899	1,739	431	6 5	5 9	14 8	8 9	2 2
1985	202,463	1,527	0 75	2,991	1,820	353	7 5	5 8	14 7	9 0	1 7
1987	205,490	1,534	0 75	2,992	1,843	386	7 4	5 6	14 5	8 9	1 9
1988	207,024	1,580	0 76	3,084	1,887	383	7 6	5 8	14 8	9 1	1 8
1989	208,604	1,617	0 78	3,105	1,872	383	7 7	5 9	14 8	8 9	1 8
BLACK											
1970	22,617	424	1 87	575	226	39	18 6	15 3	25 2	9 9	1 7
1975	24,602	382	1 55	512	218	38	15 4	11 8	20 6	8 8	1 5
1980	26,645	488	1 83	590	233	76	18 1	13 3	21 9	8 7	2 8
1985	28,802	421	1 46	608	244	58	14 5	12 5	21 0	8 4	2 0
1987	29,656	454	1 53	642	255	67	15 2	12 9	21 5	8 5	2 3
1988	30,110	452	1 50	650	259	60	14 9	12 9	21 4	8 5	2 0
1989	30,562	485	1 59	681	256	60	15 8	13 8	22 1	8 3	2 0
OTHER RACES											
1970	2,540	143	5 62	68	13	73	54 8	21 0	26 1	5 1	27 8
1975	3,375	324	9 61	81	15	238	91 0	18 5	22 6	4 1	66 8
1980	4,664	823	17 64	124	18	338	155.7	20 0	23 5	3 5	64 0
1985	6,942	377	5 43	161	23	239	52 9	19 3	22 8	3 3	33 6
1987	7,694	380	4 94	175	25	230	48 2	19 0	22 3	3 2	29 2
1988	8,074	377	4 67	179	26	224	45 7	18 6	21 7	3 1	27 1
1989	8,451	402	4 76	190	27	239	46.5	18 9	22 0	3 1	27 6

[1] Includes overseas admissions into, less discharges from, Armed Forces and includes for 1960-1980 "error of closure" (the amount necessary to make the components of change add to the net change between censuses), for which figures are not shown separately. [2] Percent of population at beginning of period. [3] Adjusted for underregistration prior to April 1, 1970. [4] Change in population by race includes the effect of a change in the definition of race.

Source: U.S. Bureau of the Census, Current Population Reports, series P-25, Nos. 1045 and 1057.

No. 15. Projections of the Hispanic Population, by Age and Sex: 1995 to 2010

[As of July 1. Includes Armed Forces overseas. See text, section 1 for explanation of methodology. Data are for the middle series with the following assumptions about fertility (ultimate lifetime births per woman), mortality (ultimate life expectancy in 2080) and immigration (yearly net immigration): 1.9 births per woman, 81.0 years, and 143,000 net immigration. These projections are not consistent with those shown in tables 16, 17, and 18. They were also prepared prior to the release of 1990 census results and are therefore not based on 1990 census data]

AGE AND SEX	POPULATION (1,000)				PERCENT DISTRIBUTION		PERCENT CHANGE	
	1995	2000	2005	2010	2000	2010	1990-2000	2000-2010
Total	22,550	25,223	27,960	30,795	100.0	100.0	26.8	22.1
Under 5 years old	2,412	2,496	2,644	2,852	9 9	9 3	9 4	14 3
5-17 years old	5,555	6,207	6,551	6,848	24 6	22 2	28 6	10 3
18-24 years old	2,511	2,787	3,254	3,599	11 0	11 7	15 9	30 1
25-34 years old	3,717	3,804	4,036	4,526	15 1	14 7	4 8	19 0
35-44 years old	3,430	3,803	3,894	3,963	15 1	12 9	36 4	4 7
45-54 years old	2,165	2,811	3,440	3,606	11 1	12 4	68 5	35 4
55-64 years old	1,342	1,619	2,093	2,704	6 4	8 8	36 9	67 0
65-74 years old	894	1,041	1,183	1,432	4 1	4 7	47 2	37 6
75 years old and over	525	678	864	1,045	2 7	3 4	61 8	54 1
16 years old and over	15,322	17,419	19,753	22,131	69 0	71 9	29 5	27 1
Male	11,285	12,627	14,000	15,419	50 1	50 1	26 9	22 1
Female	11,265	12,596	13,980	15,376	49 9	49 9	26 7	22 1

Source: U.S. Bureau of the Census, Current Population Reports, series P-25, No. 995.

No. 18. Projections of the Total Population by Age, Sex, and Race: 1995 to 2010

(As of July 1. Includes Armed Forces overseas. Data are for middle series; for assumptions see headnote, table 16. For explanation of methodology, see text, section 1. Minus sign (-) indicates decrease)

AGE, SEX, AND RACE	POPULATION (1,000)				PERCENT DISTRIBUTION		PERCENT CHANGE	
	1995	2000	2005	2010	2000	2010	1990-2000	2000-2010
Total	260,138	268,266	275,604	282,575	100.0	100.0	7.1	5.3
Under 5 years old	17,799	16,898	16,611	16,899	6.3	6.0	-8.2	(Z)
5-17 years old	48,374	48,815	47,471	45,747	18.2	16.2	7.0	-6.3
18-24 years old	24,281	25,231	26,918	27,155	9.4	9.6	-3.5	7.6
25-34 years old	40,982	37,149	35,997	37,572	13.8	13.3	-15.4	1.1
35-44 years old	42,336	43,911	40,951	37,202	16.4	13.2	15.9	-15.3
45-54 years old	31,297	37,223	41,619	43,207	13.9	15.3	46.0	16.1
55-64 years old	21,325	24,158	29,782	35,430	9.0	12.5	13.1	46.7
65-74 years old	18,930	18,243	18,410	21,039	6.8	7.4	-0.7	15.3
75 years old and over	14,834	16,639	17,864	18,323	6.2	6.5	26.2	10.1
16 years old and over	201,016	210,134	219,301	227,390	78.3	80.5	8.9	8.2
Male, total	127,123	131,191	134,858	138,333	100.0	100.0	7.3	5.4
Under 5 years old	9,118	8,661	8,517	8,666	6.6	6.3	-8.1	0.1
5-17 years old	24,787	25,027	24,350	23,473	19.1	17.0	7.1	-6.2
18-24 years old	12,290	12,770	13,628	13,752	9.7	9.9	-3.4	7.7
25-34 years old	20,579	18,662	18,091	18,878	14.2	13.6	-15.5	1.2
35-44 years old	21,104	21,945	20,458	18,586	16.7	13.4	16.8	-15.3
45-54 years old	15,292	18,296	20,585	21,432	13.9	15.5	47.5	17.1
55-64 years old	10,149	11,557	14,321	17,173	8.8	12.4	14.4	48.6
65-74 years old	8,476	8,242	8,407	9,681	6.3	7.0	0.9	17.6
75 years old and over	5,326	6,032	6,501	6,681	4.6	4.8	28.9	10.8
16 years old and over	96,834	101,392	105,984	110,024	77.3	79.5	9.2	8.5
Female, total	133,016	137,076	140,746	144,241	100.0	100.0	7.0	5.2
Under 5 years old	8,681	8,237	8,094	8,231	6.0	5.7	-8.3	-0.1
5-17 years old	23,587	23,788	23,121	22,274	17.4	15.4	6.9	-6.4
18-24 years old	11,991	12,461	13,290	13,402	9.1	9.3	-3.6	7.6
25-34 years old	20,384	18,487	17,906	18,694	13.5	13.0	-15.4	1.1
35-44 years old	21,233	21,966	20,493	18,616	16.0	12.9	14.9	-15.3
45-54 years old	16,005	18,927	21,034	21,775	13.8	15.1	44.7	15.0
55-64 years old	11,175	12,601	15,441	18,257	9.2	12.7	11.9	44.9
65-74 years old	10,454	10,001	10,004	11,348	7.3	7.9	-2.0	13.5
75 years old and over	9,507	10,607	11,364	11,642	7.7	8.1	24.7	9.8
16 years old and over	104,184	108,742	113,317	117,366	79.3	81.4	8.6	7.9
White, total	216,820	221,514	225,424	228,978	100.0	100.0	5.2	3.4
Under 5 years old	14,251	13,324	12,936	13,064	6.0	5.7	-10.5	-1.8
5-17 years old	38,493	38,569	37,118	35,258	17.4	15.4	5.6	-8.6
18-24 years old	19,452	19,988	21,188	21,298	9.0	9.3	-6.2	6.5
25-34 years old	33,680	29,988	28,603	29,585	13.5	12.9	-18.11	-1.3
35-44 years old	35,635	36,574	33,639	29,997	16.5	13.1	13.2	-18.0
45-54 years old	26,879	31,618	34,911	35,880	14.3	15.7	44.0	13.4
55-64 years old	18,327	20,667	25,407	29,913	9.3	13.1	10.9	44.7
65-74 years old	16,681	15,811	15,706	17,875	7.1	7.8	-3.5	13.1
75 years old and over	13,421	14,965	15,914	16,108	6.8	7.0	25.1	7.6
16 years old and over	169,685	175,579	181,478	186,417	79.3	81.4	6.8	6.2
Male	106,385	108,774	110,785	112,610	49.1	49.2	5.4	3.5
Female	110,455	112,739	114,639	116,366	50.9	50.8	4.9	3.2
Black, total	33,190	35,128	37,063	38,833	100.0	100.0	12.8	10.6
Under 5 years old	2,790	2,748	2,764	2,820	7.8	7.3	-2.3	2.6
5-17 years old	7,697	7,895	7,869	7,809	22.5	20.1	10.1	-1.1
18-24 years old	3,703	3,924	4,198	4,314	11.2	11.1	2.9	9.9
25-34 years old	5,534	5,264	5,299	5,590	15.0	14.4	-7.4	6.2
35-44 years old	5,041	5,481	5,332	5,076	15.6	13.1	30.2	-7.4
45-54 years old	3,261	4,108	4,828	5,369	11.7	13.8	52.9	30.8
55-64 years old	2,288	2,578	3,155	3,995	7.3	10.3	19.6	55.0
65-74 years old	1,762	1,848	1,994	2,277	5.3	5.9	14.9	23.2
75 years old and over	1,122	1,283	1,445	1,584	3.7	4.1	27.7	23.5
16 years old and over	23,880	25,708	27,638	29,467	73.2	75.9	15.7	14.6
Male	15,640	16,787	17,707	18,602	47.8	47.9	13.2	10.8
Female	17,350	18,342	19,296	20,231	52.2	52.1	12.4	10.3
Other races, total	10,119	11,624	13,177	14,764	100.0	100.0	34.5	27.0
Under 5 years old	758	826	911	995	7.1	6.7	17.8	20.4
5-17 years old	2,184	2,350	2,464	2,680	20.2	18.2	22.2	14.1
18-24 years old	1,126	1,309	1,532	1,542	11.3	10.4	31.1	17.9
25-34 years old	1,748	1,897	2,095	2,398	16.3	16.2	17.1	26.3
35-44 years old	1,660	1,856	1,980	2,129	16.0	14.4	34.5	14.7
45-54 years old	1,156	1,500	1,780	1,979	12.9	13.4	76.2	32.0
55-64 years old	711	912	1,200	1,523	7.8	10.3	59.9	67.1
65-74 years old	487	584	708	886	5.0	6.0	51.9	51.8
75 years old and over	290	391	506	632	3.4	4.3	79.3	61.8
16 years old and over	7,483	8,847	10,186	11,506	76.1	77.9	40.5	30.1
Male	4,918	5,629	6,386	7,122	48.4	48.2	33.3	26.5
Female	5,202	5,995	6,811	7,642	51.6	51.8	35.6	27.5

Z Less than .05 percent.

Source: U.S. Bureau of the Census, Current Population Reports, series P-25, No. 1018.

APPENDIX D

Data derived from the <u>Statistical Yearbook of the Immigration and Naturalization Service</u>, US Immigration and Naturalization Service (US Government Printing Office, Wash. D.C.) Years reviewed are 1984 and 1990.

Region	1984 K-1 Immigration	1990 K-1 Immigration	Numeric Difference	Percent Difference
All Country.	5641	6313	672	11.91 +
Asia	2927	3212	285	09.74 +
Philippine	1559	1702	143	09.17 +
Africa	155	183	28	18.06 +
Caribbean	134	173	39	29.15 +
Cent.Amer[2]	94	130	36	38.30 +
Europe[2]	1093	1203	110	10.06 +
Latin Amer.	278	364	86	30.94 +
Oceania[1,2]	96	121	25	26.04 +
Non Europ[2]	3684	4183	499	13.55 +

[1] Oceania refers to Australia and the South Pacific Islands excluding the Hawaiian islands.

[2] Adjustments for Austrailian, Mexican and Canadian immigration were not needed and therefore not reported here. Total numbers will therefore not equal the "All Countries" figure. However, the 13.55% figure is still accurate even when these countries are considered.

[3] The overall numbers of Non-European immigrants coming into the country as fiancee's to American citizens exceeds European immigration for the same purpose. Philippine immigration alone, exceeds European immigration under the K-1 Visa.